Praise for Scale Passion

"When I think of Rob Craven, the words 'scale' and 'passion' resonate like a Jimi Hendrix guitar solo. Businesses run well by passionate teams are the only true hope for this world. In *Scale Passion*, Rob explains how to live your purpose, love your life, and save the world."

—Patrick Sullivan Jr., CEO & Cofounder, Jigsaw Health

"You can make money with any business, but the reason behind the business will determine the impact it has for you, your employees, your customers, and the world we all share.Your purpose determines your daily experience at work. *Scale Passion* teaches entrepreneurs to infuse purpose in everything we do to drive the outcomes we want. You're much more likely to get where you want to go if you have a clear map with the destination identified. This is a must-read for business owners who give a shit."

—Andrew Brandeis, ND, Cofounder & CEO, OK Capsule

"Rob worked with our leadership team at CLG for several years doing exactly what he shares with you in this book. Rob was masterful and the principles he both taught and modeled transformed us and our organization. He knows his stuff, walks his talk, and has maps to show all of us the way."

—Jim Dethmer, Coauthor, *15 Commitments of Conscious Leadership*, and Cofounder, Conscious Leadership Group

"Rob Craven is a longtime friend who exudes a passion for empowering business leaders that is rarely seen. He has an uncanny ability to jump into your business and offer vision and insights as if it's his own. *Scale Passion* is a user-friendly guide to take your company from a business to a true platform that can benefit and bless everyone involved from employees to vendors to customers. If you want to scale your passion and run your business on purpose, you found the right resource."

—Jordan Rubin, Founder, Garden of Life, Beyond Organic, Ancient Nutrition, and *New York Times Bestselling* Author, *The Maker's Diet*

"Robert Craven's *Scale Passion* has been a transformative force for Total Fire Protection. He doesn't just offer advice; he equips leaders with the tools to foster a culture of passion and excellence within their organizations. If you're serious about taking your business to the next level, *Scale Passion* is a must-read, and Craven's coaching is an experience that will resonate long after you've turned the final page."

—Joseph Capone, Chief Executive Officer & Cofounder,
Total Fire Protection

"Being able to tap into one's personal passion creates an unrivaled source of energy, spirit, and business charisma that propels leaders forward. In *Scale Passion*, Robert has identified not just the sauce, but a "secret jet fuel" in a way that's both accessible and inspirational! I've seen these concepts in-place in my own businesses over dozens of years, and I can attest that these concepts greatly increase odds of success—and make the journey a lot more fun!"

—Rod Harl, Chairman, Alene Candles

"I've been a passionate social entrepreneur for over two decades. *Scale Passion* is the first business book I've read that helped me pave the path forward to realizing my purpose with impact-driven business ventures. The practical steps are spot on and there is incredible wisdom in these pages. I wish I found this book earlier on my journey to help avoid common pitfalls that cost time, money, heartache, and failure. Highly recommended!"

Jamie Bianchini, Cofounder & CEO, Purpose In Expenses

"*Scale Passion* by Rob Craven is a game-changer in the world of leadership. The way Rob dives into the concept of harnessing energy is both inspiring and practical. His insights have shown me how to channel my energy into a focused, purpose-driven strategy, leading to personal growth, becoming a stronger leader, and cultivating a thriving business culture."

Jeff Byers, CEO & Cofounder of Momentous

"I have benefited firsthand from Rob Craven's powerful model for clarifying and scaling passion. Having Rob and his strategic wisdom on your team or on your bookshelf is like having a superpower for growing your business and understanding why you do what you do."

—Doug Abrams, CEO, Idea Architects Book and Media Agency,
and *New York Times* Bestselling Coauthor,
The Book of Joy and *The Book of Hope*

"The information in this book is not theory but born out of decades of experience by a lifelong learner who is passionate about seeing others reach their full potential and live with meaning. Rob's real-world examples are both inspiring and practical. I highly recommend *Scale Passion* for anyone looking to scale their business while staying true to their values."

—Aaron E. Bartz, Chief Strategy Officer and former President, Ortho Molecular Products

"I love Rob Craven's book. What a gift this is to everyone working on their personal success story. I have been in the nutritional products field as a business founder and innovator for more than 40 years. This book does a better job in the creation of a road map to success—not only in business but life—than any I have ever read over these four decades. It is infused in passion, and delivers a powerful recipe for success. It is a book that I will continue to read for years to come as inspiration."

—Jeffrey Bland, PhD, former President, Metagenics; Founder, Institute for Functional Medicine; and Founder, Big Bold Health

"As entrepreneurs, most of us ultimately want to build a company that not only delivers exceptional products or services but also makes a real difference in the world. *Scale Passion* provides the blueprint for doing just that. Rob's Scale Passion Method, pulled from his own incredible achievements in business, is a practical guide for integrating your particular passion with a practical business strategy. Packed with real-world examples, *Scale Passion*s hows you how to build a company where purpose drives profit and every decision contributes to a larger goal. Ultimately, how to build a company that actually matters."

—Tom Blue, Healthcare Entrepreneur

SCALE PASSION

SCALE PASSION

A Blueprint for Building Purpose-Driven Businesses

Igniting Purpose, Driving Impact

ROB CRAVEN
with DAVE MOORE

Matt Holt Books
An Imprint of BenBella Books, Inc.
Dallas, TX

Matt Holt is an imprint of BenBella Books, Inc.
8080 N. Central Expressway
Suite 1700
Dallas, TX 75206
benbellabooks.com
Send feedback to feedback@benbellabooks.com

BenBella and *Matt Holt* are federally registered trademarks.

Printed in the United States of America
10 9 8 7 6 5 4 3 2 1

Library of Congress Control Number: 2024034202
ISBN 9781637746417 (hardcover)
ISBN 9781637746424 (electronic)

Editing by Katie Dickman
Copyediting by Jessica Easto
Proofreading by Michael Fedison and Marissa Wold Uhrina
Text design and composition by Jordan Koluch
Cover design by Brigid Pearson
Printed by Sheridan MI

For Lew Craven
1946–2021

Contents

Stage 3: Radiate Purpose and Impact

A note on lexicon: Whether you are a founder, entrepreneur, business owner, CEO, or executive, you will benefit from this book. However, for clarity and concision, I will refer to all of you as the change-the-world business owner, or business owner, because I want you to adopt the change-the-world owner mindset. The owner mindset is passionate, purposeful, adaptive, resilient, and always all in. The greatest compliment I can give you professionally is saying, "You think like an owner." So whether you're a solopreneur, team lead, nonprofit director, or the CEO of a $6 billion company, welcome.

Introduction

Make a Difference. Be Bold. Do It Right.

Sometimes it takes a little inspiration to light a fire. So who inspires you? Who's your hero? My hero is easy to name: my dad, Lew Craven. And he inspired me at a young age. My parents married in their late teens, and in 1973 at the age of 25, my dad went to work at an up-and-coming company called Eastern Airlines, where he worked his way from the cleaning crew to ramp rat (loading baggage into the plane's belly) and other positions.

He moved around a lot, but my mom and I stayed put, flying to visit him from time to time, which was always exciting. When I was growing up, my dad always took the lead carving pumpkins at Halloween. One year, we didn't have a pumpkin, so he carved one from his post in Washington, DC, and, enlisting his ramp rat buddies, shipped it all the way to Charlotte, North Carolina, where we picked it up. That was cool, but it wasn't the stuff of real heroism.

But this is: When I was six years old, my dad's cancer reached a stage where he was given only a few years to live. So he decided, right then and there, that he had 27 years of wisdom to pour into his only child in a short time. He taught me practical skills like shaving (albeit without a blade!), and he taught me how to conduct myself, which included three maxims to live by. The first maxim was to *always make a difference* in whatever you do. Make an impact. The second was to *be bold as hell*, although I think I added the "as hell" part over the years. And the third maxim was to *always do it right*. Don't go through the motions or do the bare minimum.

When he passed his lifetime's accumulated wisdom on to me, I was too young to fully register its meaning, much less live my life in accordance with it. But as I grew older and went out into the world, the maxims served me every step of the way and shaped who I have become. After graduating from the University of Florida with a business degree, I began to forge a career at some top companies, such as Procter & Gamble and Boston Scientific. These organizations were renowned for their training programs, and I learned a lot about sales, marketing, and business strategy working in them.

But I also learned what I didn't care for in certain kinds of businesses. They were too buttoned-down, to risk averse, and above all, too shareholder focused for a young buck who still had his father's encouragements to make a difference ringing in his ears. I went to work as the vice president of sales and marketing at e-Builder, one of the first online B2B companies, early in the dot-com explosion. I learned some important lessons there, not least of all about failed ownership equity promises. So, I made a momentous decision, one that felt especially bold given I was a newlywed, and went into business with a partner as a consultant, a role in which I advised companies as big as Kmart and Clorox and brought category management to retailers that had little to no category data. My partner and I helped them capture data in new ways. We sold this firm, and I went to work for the Hackett Group, which is where I learned business best practices in a deep way by interviewing the top leaders at places like IBM and Textron.

At the same time, not being a golfer while living in the golf mecca of Palm Beach Gardens, Florida, I spent my spare time helping entrepreneurs get their businesses off the ground. One of those entrepreneurs was

Jordan Rubin, the founder of the whole-food supplement maker Garden of Life. There, as an early friend and eventually as CEO, I partnered with Jordan to lead the company by setting bold and difference-making goals and objectives. We'll talk more about my work with Jordan in a later chapter, but my experience at Garden of Life led to my working at another consumer-packaged goods (CPG) company called MegaFood, a true innovator with a deep history, based in New Hampshire. More importantly, MegaFood had a deep commitment to farming, nutrition, and manufacturing supplements out of whole foods grown from the earth. If Garden of Life put me firmly on the road to living out my dad's advice to be bold, make a difference, and do it right, MegaFood was where I learned just how far such a road might lead.

While at MegaFood, I experienced two things that proved transformative in my development as an impact-focused leader. The first was being chosen from many applicants to attend a course at Harvard Business School on creating shared value, taught by the well-respected business school professor Michael Porter. The course included participants from over 30 countries, and some of the companies represented in the room were BP, the Bill & Melinda Gates Foundation, Amgen, Mitsubishi, Toyota, and Nike. The chairman of Nestlé even flew in from Switzerland to participate in one of our case studies.

The experience was transformative for me, and I remain convinced that the future of business lies in applying the shared value principles in practice. So, what is creating shared value? Let me share a passage from the original 2011 *Harvard Business Review* article "Creating Shared Value," in which Michael E. Porter and Mark R. Kramer advance the idea:

> Companies must take the lead and bring business and society back together. The solution lies in the principle of shared value, which involves creating economic value in a way that also creates value for society by addressing its needs and challenges ... Shared value is not social

responsibility, philanthropy, or even sustainability, but a new way to achieve economic success.

The authors go on to offer hypothetical examples of how shared value would work in the real world, including one in the fair-trade movement. Fair trade, say the authors, "aims to increase the proportion of revenue that goes to poor farmers by paying them higher prices for the same crops." The authors contrast this practice with a shared value perspective focus "on strengthening the local cluster of supporting suppliers and other institutions in order to increase farmers' efficiency, yields, product quality, and sustainability. This leads to a bigger pie of revenue and profits that benefits both farmers and the companies that buy from them."

At the individual company level, I understand this to mean that how you operate, who you buy from and sell to, who you hire and promote, and how responsive you are to your community's needs can create shared value. Creating shared value in your community doesn't cut into your profits because you need a strong community around to be a strong company. In fact, if you are protecting a premium position, this approach will help because everybody is making more money.

At MegaFood, we had already begun applying the principles of shared value in our practices by paying a living wage, earning recognition as a Best Place to Work multiple times, and becoming an indispensable partner to family farms across the country. On a personal level, I won conscious leadership awards and became a featured speaker in my industry known for being a leader in growth, transparency, and building award-winning cultures, all while making a difference in the world and building a fast-growing company that went on to sell to a larger company for the highest multiple of EBITDA in our segment at the time.

In partnership with Ben & Jerry's and Patagonia, we raised more than the 30 thousand signatures needed to get a law passed to get the carcinogen glyphosate banned as a desiccant on oats. Closer to home, we planted community gardens with local immigrant populations in the city of Manchester, New Hampshire, where MegaFood is based. And while we grew the company fivefold during my tenure, we also successfully applied for B Corp status, thus affirming our commitment to profitable growth and social impact.

Were our initiatives perfectly executed in every instance? Of course not. But you can't make a difference and do things right if you aren't bold. And you can't be bold if you don't court a setback or failure or two along the way that you can learn from. But our successes far outweighed our setbacks, and by the time I left MegaFood to create my own companies, the business was a highly visible and impactful presence in the Granite State and the entire natural products industry.

The second transformative experience was reading Peter Diamandis's 2012 bestseller, *Abundance: The Future Is Better Than You Think*. In it, Diamandis argues that exponential technological growth in computing, energy, medicine, and many other areas will soon enable an unprecedented abundance that today seems impossible. Billions of people around the world will enjoy greater access to food, clean water, health care, education, and many other things that will improve their lives. The book offers plenty of examples of recent breakthroughs, so it wasn't an exercise in futurism but rather a report from the cutting edge of innovation.

I attended Diamandis's Abundance360 Summit and heard directly from the inventors, thinkers, entrepreneurs, and technology visionaries who were calling for "moonshot" solutions to the world's problems. Within this model, aiming for the moon replaces traditional incremental measures of progress—say, 10% annually—with exponential measures of progress more like 10 times!

At first glance, this kind of transformative change can seem audacious and even hubristic, but the word that most aptly describes it is probably *urgent.* A moonshot is something you launch with your whole soul. At MegaFood, our mission of ending nutritional poverty was a bona fide moonshot. We just hadn't known it—at least not as such.

I can honestly say that when I left MegaFood at the end of 2018 after 11 amazing years, I got a glimpse of what it means to build a company that is making an impact in the world. This is where I learned to tap into my energy and purpose and support others in doing the same to become not only empowered but also responsible to our mission and our purpose. Since that time, I have seen this energy emanate from individuals both in small and profound ways: a teammate who discovered her passion and zone of genius and moved on to prominent positions in other companies, the farmers and retailers we partnered with, and the communities we touched through our effort to limit glyphosate.

This experience of our moonshot stayed with me and profoundly influenced the missions of my next companies, Findaway Adventures, which I founded along with my partners, Brian and Chris, and now ScalePassion. It also informs the narrative structure of the book you are now reading.

Leadership Begins with Your Purpose

One of the key tenets of this book is that before you can build and scale a change-the-world company, you must become a great leader of others, and before you do that, you must first harness your personal purpose and learn to lead yourself. I felt sure I was meant to lead others as far back as my days at P&G, but the kind of leader I wanted to be took longer for me to discover—about as long as it took me to really tap into my personal purpose.

Early in my tenure with MegaFood, I began working with the Conscious Leadership Group and became committed to the 15 Commitments of Conscious Leadership. Through the group's emphasis on deep self-knowledge and a commitment to integrity, I realized that I am at my best when I am teaching, coaching, aligning, and inspiring. That's my superpower, and my current passion is to help impact-minded business owners scale their personal impact while using their companies to create even broader impact.

This was the mission of the third company I cofounded, Findaway Adventures, an investment incubator, and my current business, ScalePassion, a consulting firm dedicated to helping business owners who want to scale their impact.

What does it mean to scale impact? Well, think about the idea of scaling a business. In general, it refers to our ability to grow and expand a company while maintaining efficiency and profitability. A company that scales its sales capacity might be able to increase revenues without significantly increasing its costs or workforce. My passion in life is to help business owners bake social impact into their companies from the very beginning so that as their businesses grow and flourish, so does their impact. And if enough business owners in organizations large, medium, and small can learn how to scale their impact, we can effect a tipping point in the current practice of capitalism.

Evolving Capitalism

I am neither an advocate of socialism—not by a long shot—nor an advocate for greater government control of business or investment in more nongovernmental organizations. But I am suggesting, emphatically, that capitalism has reached a point where it needs to evolve, and the best place to do so is at its source: the business owners who collectively wield enormous power and unlimited potential to put the resources of good business to better use for all the people who share our planet.

Capitalism has had a long and world-shaping career since its earliest days in 16th-century mercantilism and the rise of colonialism. From these beginnings to the industrial age of the 18th and 19th centuries to the rise of finance capitalism in the 20th century, the growing influence of banks, stock markets, monopolies, and trusts created enormous wealth that, while not shared equally among people and places, nonetheless improved the lives of billions of people worldwide.

Regardless of which one of these phases or stages of capitalism prevailed, all proceeded from the belief that the sole purpose of business creation was creating private wealth. In 1970, the economist Milton Friedman codified this belief in an essay for the *New York Times* called "A Friedman Doctrine: The Social Responsibility of Business Is to Increase Its Profits." In the article, he argued that a company and its executives have no social responsibility to the public or society, only to their shareholders: "In a free-enterprise, private-property system, a corporate executive is an employee of the owners of the business. He has direct responsibility to his employers. That responsibility is to conduct the business in accordance with their desires . . . the key point is that, in his capacity as a corporate executive, the manager is the agent of the individuals who own the corporation . . . and his primary responsibility is to them."

Every dollar of profit redirected toward social causes, wrote Friedman, was a dollar taken from a shareholder, and every price increase intended to pay for the cost associated with social action was a dollar taken from customers.

By the later decades of the 20th century to the present day, however, capitalism in its various permutations—influenced by globalism, technology, and the expanding power of financial institutions—has raised questions about the next phase of capitalism and whether Friedman's single-stakeholder model needs to be challenged. Not with socialism and central control, but with a wider embrace of new stakeholders whose well-being is critical to business success in the long term. Today, many business owners are concerned about the lack of progress our country has made on important issues, such as human health and wellness, environmental changes, and economic justice. With politics mired in partisanship, the business community is looking inward to explore ways to create change. Many business owners are already making headway; their stories of using business to improve lives as well as make a profit are truly inspirational.

The problems are not unknown and have been the subject of many books, scholarly articles, podcasts, and business biographies that have explored the troubling aspect of this age of so-called late capitalism: business's focus on shareholder returns supersedes every other consideration, including the prosperity of businesses' own employees, the economic health of the communities in which businesses operate, and the health of the natural environment that sustains all of us.

It doesn't have to be this way. In fact, it cannot long continue to be this way. So, our challenge is to begin to set the table for capitalism to evolve into something more sustainable for all people in all places.

From Output to Impact

Not long ago, I listened to a presentation by UBS Chief Economist Paul Donovan in which he spoke of an economic shift taking place in the past few years, marked by the shift from a focus on satisfying needs and desires through the *output* of goods and services to one that increasingly focuses on social and environmental *impact* as well as basic needs. In many ways, the impact economy has emerged as a corrective to the excesses and short-term thinking of the output economy.

There is a growing body of work addressing this shift toward purpose or corporate social responsibility. The phrase *purpose driven* has popped up everywhere in books and corporate branding materials to connote a business's commitment to something deeper than its bottom line, no matter how shallow that commitment may be. Often, when people think of impact, they think of health food stores and billionaires buying up vast tracts of land or pouring resources into pet projects or philanthropies.

The problem is that while those examples of impact can produce real, great, practical, and inspirational value, they represent only a fraction of businesses trying to make a difference in the world. These are the many small to medium companies that quietly and earnestly use or seek to use business to make an impact with their products and services. They are usually operating below the radar.

How do I know this? I work with them every day. They number in the hundreds of thousands. You haven't heard of most of them. They produce hardware, software, home construction components, vitamin subscription services, applesauce, bodywash. You name it! You'll meet some of them in this book. (Their stories are real, but the names and details have been changed unless we received specific permission to share them.)

I've witnessed the most common mistakes they make and helped them develop the necessary strategic and leadership platforms to surmount their setbacks and create successful, growing, impact-focused companies. As a founder, investor, consultant, and CEO many times over, I've learned to connect the dots between product and purpose, so to speak, and have created a methodology—the Scale Passion Method—that can be applied regardless of your size, industry, or experience to grow your impact as you grow your company.

A Focus on the How

This book outlines why you should and how you can use your business for good, especially in the early stages, when so much can derail you from realizing your purpose. Through real-life examples of well-known and little-known businesses, the chapters ahead point out the most common mistakes business owners make and offer proven methods for becoming a successful change-the-world business owner and building an impact-minded organization.

That's right. This is a how-to book that offers practical, tactical advice, illustrations, examples, and links to tools you can use to ensure that your purpose continues to grow as your business grows. And if enough of us can adopt the Scale Passion Method to sufficient degrees, we can effect a tipping point that will produce real, systemic, and lasting improvement in our capitalistic society.

So, where do you start?

Don't Read This Book. Use It.

If you're a founder or CEO, you've already learned that it's lonely at the top. You're a peer of no one at your company, forced to swallow your fear and frustration and doubt and soldier on to keep your team soldiering on because as the business owner goes, so goes the business!

The good news is you don't have to soldier on alone. I encourage you to view this book as a field manual shared with you by a companion who has walked in your shoes and looked across the conference table at the same (choose one: uncomprehending, bored, resistant, resentful) faces of (employees, investors, customers, suppliers) staring back at you. One who knows your pain but also knows how you should and shouldn't react to that pain to achieve long-term success.

I wrote this book for three groups of business leaders: founders or entrepreneurs, CEOs, and leaders of teams. That may seem like a large group to gather under a single tent, but its members share a common leadership trajectory that I model on the flight of a rocket ship. (Although I've never been an astronaut, I have launched companies into orbit, so I believe the analogy works!) To see what I mean and where you may be at this point in your leadership trajectory, here are the three stages of flight that form the structure of this book:

- **Stage 1:** Elevate your personal leadership and strategy from the core by leveraging your very personal purpose, passion, and power. Discover the four superpowers of leadership and *your* zone of genius and energy source, learning how to channel them toward building a strategic platform that is clear, purpose driven, and universally inspiring.
- **Stage 2:** Scale your purpose and passion by building a team and leading others in executing your strategy. Your passion as a business owner is infectious because your team looks to you for direction and inspiration. This stage shows how you can develop a community of responsible business owners and operational standards that will enable your team to execute your strategy and purpose with increasing independence.
- **Stage 3:** Inspire an ever-widening circle of customers, investors, community members, and other stakeholders. A business owner's energy is difficult to maintain throughout the lifespan of a company. This stage shows you how to (re)capture and articulate your passion and purpose for others to run with, whether you continue to lead the company or have moved on to a new project. This stage is all about developing an impact culture in your business that can survive (and thrive) independently from you.

Where do you stand in terms of developing your purpose-driven, high-impact leadership? Do any of these stages sound familiar to you right now? The fastest way to gauge where you are is to take our online assessment at www.areyoureadytoscale.com.

We have written the chapters so that they may either be read

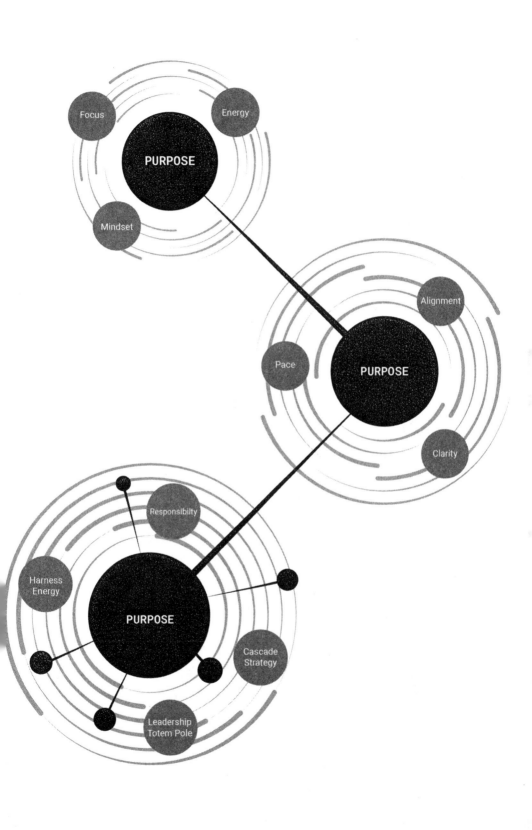

sequentially as a full six-quarter trip to Jupiter or serve as stand-alone reference points for any of the dozens of steps, challenges, and milestones you'll encounter during the scaling process.

If you're already a master or maven of the Scale Passion mindset, use the book as a training tool for members of your team. I did this at the companies I led, cascading these principles out to my senior leaders, then to the broader leadership team, and finally, to the entire company.

As you read the stories and apply the lessons in this book, remember that industry research is sending us an unequivocal message about becoming bolder with our impact. For example:

- **Social impact is a differentiator with consumers:** If all things are equal, or even if your product might be priced a little higher, industry data suggests that consumers are more likely to pick a company that's doing good in the world over one that isn't. Nielson research (See "2015 Nielson Global Sustainability Report") found that "66 percent of global respondents say they're willing to pay more for products and services that come from companies that are committed to positive social and environmental impact."
- **Social impact is an employee engagement powerhouse:** In the "2018 Deloitte Global Human Capital Trends" report, Deloitte found that employees who experienced a sense of purpose and meaning in their work and felt it aligned with a broader mission or purpose were more likely to be passionate about their jobs, go the extra mile, and stay at the company. Leading with purpose also attracted more talented employees.
- **Social impact is a prized asset for investors:** The Global Sustainable Investment Alliance (GSIA) publishes a biennial report titled "Global Sustainable Investment Review" that has consistently shown a rising trend in sustainable investing, indicating that

companies focusing on social impact are more valuable to investors or big strategic firms.

So, what do you think? Are you ready to make a difference, be bold, and do it right? Are you ready for liftoff?

Author's Note

You might be wondering why we named the book *Scale Passion* when it's really all about purpose. Here is the answer: passion is a strong and barely controllable emotion. I define *purpose* as a clear and compelling reason for being that drives you to make a meaningful impact in the world, aligning your values, passions, and actions toward a significant goal. To me, a business owner needs to plug into their purpose with the same energy they would feel passion.

Lew's Tips & Resources

Remember, my dad Lew's first maxim was to always *make a difference* in whatever you do. Don't go through the motions or do the minimum. Make an impact. The second was to *be bold as hell*. And the third maxim was to *do it right*. With this in mind, I will be recommending some resources at the end of each chapter that are designed to inspire you in a way that would make Lew proud.

At this point in our time together, it is important that you are inspired to move forward. Gathering evidence around how other inspired business owners have paved the way will increase your confidence to *be bold* and intent on *making a difference*! More on *doing it right* follows in the coming chapters.

Maxim 1: Make a Difference

Don't just go through the motions or settle for the minimum. Strive to have an impact in whatever you do.

Maxim 2: Be Bold

Take risks and push the boundaries. Don't be afraid to step outside of your comfort zone to achieve your goals.

Maxim 3: Do It Right

Focus on quality and integrity in everything you do. Take the time to ensure that your actions align with your values and make a positive contribution to the world.

I stand on the shoulders of many authors, mentors, and thought leaders who made me the man and leader that I am. At the end of each chapter, I will recommend resources that inspired me and might allow you to take your learning to a new level. You can always find a simple list of these resources at www.scalepassion.com/resources.

Further Reading

- "Creating Shared Value" by Michael Porter and Mark Kramer
- *Conscious Capitalism* by John Mackey and Raj Sisodia
- *Abundance* by Peter Diamandis and Steven Kotler
- *10x Is Easier Than 2x* by Dan Sullivan and Dr. Benjamin Hardy

Scale Passion Resources

- "Are You Ready to Scale?" assessment: a simple, online survey that will help you map your gaps to scaling purpose
- "A Scorecard for the Change-the-World Leader": map your personal leadership journey of scaling purpose

Stage 1

HARNESS YOUR PURPOSE AND LEAD YOURSELF

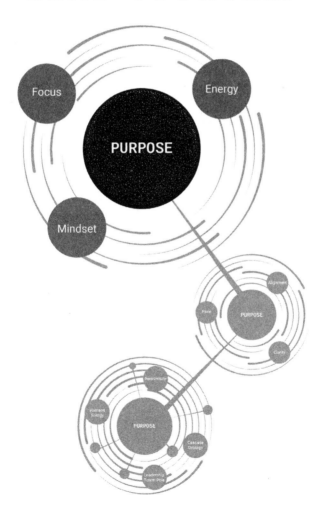

Chapter 1

Impact Is Your Decision to Make. What's Holding You Back?

L ong before *Forbes* designated Ethan Holmes as one of its 30 Under 30 business leaders and innovators and long before Bloomberg, PBS, Fox, and Black Enterprise started covering his company, Ethan was a kid who loved eating his grandfather's applesauce.

Ethan knew from an early age that he wanted to be an entrepreneur. In 2005, at the age of 15, he launched his first venture from the family kitchen: Holmes Made Foods. He made candy bars and told people he was going to be "the next Willy Wonka of Cleveland." When he realized he couldn't make candy bars that would drive the local Oompa Loompas wild, he pivoted by tapping into a cherished childhood memory—his grandfather's culinary skills—and his entrepreneurial spirit.

"He lived with us and made a lot of great food from scratch," Ethan said of his grandfather Elmer Buford, whose many culinary specialties included homemade applesauce. In 2008, Holmes asked Mr. Buford to teach him the recipe.

Ethan found inspiration in a deeply personal memory that fueled his entrepreneurial interests. I first met Ethan when he was in a pitch slam, and I was one of the investor-judges. Ethan's pitch was rather conventional. He followed all the norms an entrepreneur is supposed to follow, which included market potential, his product's uniqueness, and the rest. But he didn't talk at all about himself. Like so many entrepreneurs, Ethan was too humble about the passion that drove him and the larger purpose he wanted to fulfill. So, he embraced sameness rather than uniqueness.

At one point, I asked him to tell us about himself, and that's when he told us the story of his grandfather and how he wanted to use his business to help other entrepreneurs in underserved communities.

I told Ethan we'd invest in him, but only if he put his story and purpose on his packaging and all his messaging. We made the investment, and I worked with Ethan when he was rebranding his company in 2020 and learning the ropes of taking his business from Greater Cleveland to a national audience. Yes, Ethan poured himself into learning about fundraising, and he raised several hundred thousand dollars to finance his expansion. And, yes, he learned how to increase his profit by reducing his expenses in his supply chains and packaging. But all the while he sharpened his professional tool kit, he kept his purpose in the front of his mind.

And what was that purpose? Introducing the Holmes Entrepreneur Initiative.

The initiative connects Ethan's company with nonprofit partners to teach young aspiring business owners like Ethan entrepreneurial principles. Ethan constantly visits schools and community centers to inspire the next generation of entrepreneurs in underserved communities to raise their gaze to what is possible. "I was a young entrepreneur, and it was so hard for me to get started," Ethan said. "I'm very active in working with entrepreneurs in general because I know how hard it is. And I feel like I've had a lot of opportunities that I can now just give to people. You can't be scared to tell your story, take risks, and be unapologetically *you*."

Making applesauce that people would buy may have been Ethan

Holmes's great passion, but mentoring other Black entrepreneurs emerged as his purpose. We'll explore the difference between passion and purpose in chapter 2, but the point is you can choose to devote yourself to leading a business that makes a difference at any time, but the earlier you do it, the better. This chapter explores ways you can uncover the personal experiences and social concerns that have made you who you are today—even if you are initially unaware of them. The connection between your purpose and your product often arises where you'd least expect.

The Game Is Rigged

In the United States, we celebrate the self-made entrepreneur, but the truth is that the game is rigged. There is much in our culture and society, and even ourselves, that seeks to keep us in line, frustrating the boldness required to create something entirely new. Advertising, social media, and major mainstream media platforms and their 24-hour news cycles are designed to keep us living in a state of anxiety, doubt, and outright fear.

Our own physiology is complicit in keeping us in line. One of the most powerful parts of our brains is the amygdala, which has helped us mitigate risk for millennia by controlling our fabled fight, flight, or freeze response to threats. At one time, our "lizard brain" alerted us to the signs that a saber-toothed cat was patrolling the area and sent us scurrying back to the cave; today, it makes us cautious and risk averse, even when there are no saber-toothed cats outside the cave. Today, we might run from a perceived threat that is actually an opportunity. The only threat is that the opportunity may disrupt our current level of comfort.

If you want to be a change-the-world—I broadly define *change-the-world* to mean "produce a significant positive impact on"—business owner, you have to reprogram yourself to leave the comfort of the cave. But that's hard to do in today's version of capitalistic society in which, if you attend a public school, you likely spend the first 12 years of your life going through a curricular assembly line of English, math, science, and social studies. This curriculum was originally intended to prepare you for specific vocations or to take it a step further and actually attend vocational schools that are the legacy of Henry Ford's revolutionary leadership of Ford Motor and the assembly line method of mass production.

Of course, there's absolutely nothing wrong with preparing to have a career in a trade or industrial occupation. But the intensively skills-based and efficiency-minded approach to delivering education—just think of the bells that alert students to the beginning and end of each shift, er, class—does not train students in divergent thinking or the soft skills they need to be bold or to collaborate with and lead others.

This low-risk approach to education is mirrored in the cultures of many or most of our big companies, the ones we find comfort in believing are "too big to fail." Though such companies may outlast the millions of small businesses that go belly-up every year, they fail in other ways, such as providing more meaningful work for their employees, more value to the communities in which they operate, and a less extractive relationship with the ground on which they stand. What is missing in such cases is a greater human scale, by which I mean a conscious intention to create meaning and value for the folks who produce, consume, and support the products and services.

Rediscover Yourself

So, how can you get out from under these fearful and discouraging influences and rediscover why you exist and what you are meant to do on this planet? How can you rediscover what makes you special, what energizes you, and what makes you feel passionately alive?

That's kind of a trick question because the answer is to commit yourself to this process of rediscovery. That's how to start, anyway. If you can't learn these things about yourself, how do you expect others to know them and sign on to your vision? How can you expect those who may have joined your company or department for the paycheck to *stay* because of your culture and purpose if you haven't first articulated these for yourself? As we'll see later, not everyone in your company will share the same passion or purpose to equal degrees. Each of us has to define our own purpose. But that's okay. A purpose-driven company is democratic, accommodating multiple mutually reinforcing passions.

The point is that purpose has a place in your business to begin with.

It all starts with you. Your personal story. Go back over your life—get out the scrapbook or digital scrapbook to assist your memory—and think about the significant events of your life. Look for a common thread to see if you could stitch together a reason for why these events happened *to you*. There is no such thing as going too far back. Here are a few examples of experiences you might consider:

- Being rewarded or punished for something
- Feeling like you were good at something or not good enough
- Receiving well-earned praise or being overlooked for your good action
- Receiving deep, unexpected appreciation for doing something that came naturally to you
- Feeling lucky or feeling life was unfair
- Feeling included and valued versus feeling excluded and voiceless

You should be able to recall four or five of these types of significant memories in your life, so write them down.

These are personal memories, but ask yourself how they might connect to the business you founded or the one you're leading. Why did you even start your business? Was it all about making money, or was there a higher purpose that you could connect to your personal history?

Harnessing Your Superpowers

One of the surest ways of unleashing your personal purpose is to harness the four superpowers, which include purpose, energy, focus, and mindset. All of us possess these powers, but far fewer of us apply ourselves to developing them into full-blown superpowers. The following chapters in this stage of the book will explore in greater depth how you can accomplish this, but here is a quick rundown of each superpower:

- **Purpose:** Your purpose is the core superpower. It's the first among equals. It's the molten core that holds the other superpowers in its orbit. It's the reason why you do something, strive to improve, be the best, and leave the world a better place. Can you imagine if school was more oriented to helping young people identify their purpose early on and building their life around it? How much more impact would we see in the world?

- **Energy:** Your energy is the strength and enthusiasm—I prefer the word *passion*—you exhibit in your day-to-day life. When you are doing something you love to do, your energy is renewable and can seem limitless. Most of us learn early on what energizes us but lose sight of this precious insight as life (and work) pulls us in different directions. Lack of passion is your purpose's kryptonite!

- **Focus:** The more energy we have around what we do, the better we are able to focus on it. The more we focus on what we love and feel passionate about, the more energy we feel from it. It's a perfectly virtuous circle and the basis for all wise decisions about delegation, as we'll see later in the book.

- **Mindset:** I like to think of mindset as the coming together of your purpose, energy, and focus that makes you the one and only you. A mindset is a fundamental orientation to life, and the business owner who has their mindset mojo working will inspire everyone around them.

This last point is a key one: your superpowers may be subjective feelings on your part, but don't downplay them or their impact on your life. They will shape not only your pathway but also those around you. The superpowers attract people who tune in to your focused, high-energy frequency; they supercharge those who come within your orbit and share your purpose or activate different purposes that lie dormant in other people. It's the power of attraction at its finest!

Boldly Intentional

So, what is this road to becoming unapologetically you? One of the ways I coached Ethan, which you can apply yourself, is to become intentional about your personal purpose, focus, energy, and mindset. Dig deep into your personal history and write down a short list of things that matter to you more than anything else. Go beyond Maslow's list of basic needs, such as physical safety and comfort, and push to lead your life according to the higher-order needs, such as love, belonging, and self-actualization.

When you begin thinking deeply about the things that matter most to you, you can come up with surprising ways to connect your passion to a larger purpose. Some call it a big, hairy, audacious goal (or BHAG), the term Jim Collins and Jerry Porras coined in *Built to Last: Successful Habits of Visionary Companies*. Others call it a wildly important goal (or WIG), from *The 4 Disciplines of Execution* (4DX) by Sean Covey, Chris McChesney, and Jim Huling. I call it a *magnificent obsession*—something that is so important to me that I absolutely must do it.

My magnificent obsession is to improve the world by helping others scale their impact—on a personal level and through their companies. Everything I do emanates from this core purpose. I do this by being present, listening, providing vision, inspiring, aligning, coaching, and leading. I am relentless in my pursuit of learning and adding value to the lives and enterprises of others.

But you don't have to start with a BHAG, WIG, or magnificent obsession. You can put a smaller stake in the ground and build from there. For example, Jordan Rubin, another entrepreneur I know, started his company to help people suffering from Crohn's disease. This small step led to an incredible impact as Jordan expanded his business (we'll return to Jordan in the next chapter).

Or, you might fully explore your zone of genius—what Gay Hendricks describes in *The Big Leap* as the thing you do better than anyone else on the planet, the thing that is easy for you even though it seems so hard for others. You are doing it when you are "in the zone" or "in a flow state." Ask yourself: How much of your day involves actually *doing that thing*? I'll wager it's far less than you'd like, what with having to wear all those hats as the founder, CEO, or key leader.

It's important to put the time in to understand and articulate your zone of genius. We have assembled a comprehensive set of exercises to help you develop this and have included some exercises in Lew's Tips at the end of this chapter. I can tell you one thing for sure: once you nail your zone of genius, you will feel energized in a way you have rarely felt since you were young, when life was one big adventure yet to unfold.

Having a purpose that aligns with your life story is the biggest energy rush you can experience. Your purpose aligns with your life when you can own even the worst moments of your life as lessons that fuel your purpose. For example, when my dad was diagnosed with cancer, little did I know how impactful it was, how it would put me on to my purpose. I turned a bad memory into motivation to change the world. My mentor and colleague, Nick Van Nice, has made his life's work as a personal coach the study of aligning purpose and focus. He is particularly interested in optimizing human energy and believes a leader's energy is anchored in a deep connection to living their purpose.

"As a rule, I have found that bold and impactful business owners radiate an energy that drives them powerfully toward their mission in life. Their energy is so resonant that it lights up whatever conversation, project, or gathering they join," Nick likes to say. "If a leader's personal passion is the driving force of their organization's mission and vision, they stay energized, and it becomes highly contagious."

Nick likes to quote the Hindu philosopher Patanjali (see *The Yoga Sutras of Patanjali*), who captured the relationship between energy and purpose as articulately as anyone when he shared the following wisdom:

> When you are inspired by some great purpose, some extraordinary project, all your thoughts break their bonds. Your mind transcends limitations, your consciousness expands in every direction, and you find yourself in a new, great, and wonderful world. Dormant forces, faculties and talents become alive, and you discover yourself to be a greater person by far than you ever dreamed yourself to be.

As we'll see in a later chapter, Nick's work with business leaders has shown that a leader's personal energy management sets the tone for the team's success. And it all begins with knowing what to focus on—on what matters most.

Now, given your personal story and zone of genius, how are you personally going to improve the world?

Seriously, *you.*

The one and only you.

Lew's Tips & Resources

My dad would say that before you can truly make a difference, you will need the courage to stand up for something in this world. So, make time right now to do the work to discover your calling and clearly define this major energy source for yourself.

Maxim 1: Make a Difference

- **Uncover your personal story:** Reflect on significant events in your life and identify common threads that reveal your purpose and passion.
- **Connect personal and professional:** Explore how your personal experiences and passions align with your business goals. For example, Ethan Holmes connected his love for his grandfather's recipe with his entrepreneurial spirit.
- **Commit to rediscovery:** Make a conscious effort to rediscover what makes you unique and what energizes you. This process is essential for articulating your vision and inspiring others to join your journey.

Maxim 2: Be Bold

- **Recognize external influences:** Acknowledge the societal and cultural factors that may discourage you from pursuing bold ideas. The game might seem rigged, but awareness is the first step toward overcoming these barriers.
- **Reprogram yourself:** Challenge the fear and doubt instilled by external influences. Reprogram your mindset to embrace risk and novelty, essential qualities for change-the-world leaders.
- **Embrace divergent thinking:** Break free from the traditional

education and corporate cultures that prioritize conformity and efficiency. Cultivate divergent thinking and the soft skills necessary for bold leadership.

Maxim 3: Do It Right

- **Define your purpose:** Articulate your personal purpose and align it with your business goals. Consider adopting a BHAG or a WIG to guide your endeavors.
- **Identify your zone of genius:** Identify what you do better than anyone else and prioritize activities that align with your strengths. Spend more time in your zone of genius to maximize your impact and fulfillment.
- **Manage your energy:** Recognize the connection between personal energy and purpose. Cultivate a deep connection to your purpose to radiate energy and inspire others. Remember Patanjali's wisdom: when inspired by a great purpose, your consciousness expands and dormant talents become alive.

Books or Articles to Consider
- *Trust Me, I'm Lying: Confessions of a Media Manipulator* by Ryan Holiday
- *The 4 Disciplines of Execution* by Chris McChesney, Sean Covey, and Jim Huling

Scale Passion Resources
- "Are You Ready to Scale Your Personal Leadership?" assessment: map your opportunities for harnessing your purpose
- *Your Personal Flight Plan* workbook: a do-it-yourself guide for harnessing your personal purpose

- "Finding Your Zone of Genius" exercises: a do-it-yourself approach to defining your zone of genius

Find a comprehensive list of resources at ScalePassion.com/Resources.

Chapter 2

Superpower #1: Your Purpose

As the leader goes, so goes the business. In this book, you'll read those words more than once, so get used to them. They define the fundamental mindset of the change-the-world business owner. And the number one superpower on which the change-the-world leader stands is—drumroll—*purpose*!

People often interchange the words *passion* and *purpose*, but I believe they mean two different things. The dictionary definition describes *passion* as a powerful liking, attraction, or devotion to something; it describes *purpose* as something set up as an object or end to be attained. I prefer to use the word *purpose* because it involves the desire for change. Passion doesn't prompt you to ask why, while purpose begins with the question as its first principle.

Remember Ethan Holmes? Making applesauce that people would buy may have been Ethan's great passion, but serving as a model and mentor for other Black entrepreneurs emerged as his purpose. But he had to work hard to discover it.

In all likelihood, so do you.

In my work with business owners, I have seen many who began working with a passion for something they were good at, whether writing business plans or software, speaking in public, or rallying other people around a project. Eventually, they discovered their larger purpose through their passion for the work they excelled at. When you become good at something, the world wants what you have to offer, which can lift you onto a bigger stage than you previously thought possible.

But there is another way to access your sense of purpose: examining your life and aligning the person you have become with the difference you want to make through the work you want to do. To illustrate what I mean, let me tell you more about Jordan Rubin, someone I met years ago.

What "On Purpose" Looks Like

Growing up, Jordan had the debilitating and little-understood (at the time) condition now known as Crohn's disease. The disease made his life unpleasant enough that he dropped out of college and moved to California, where he'd heard about some people working on substances and techniques that could help him treat his condition. When we met in the late 1990s, he and his wife and a small handful of others were selling little bags of black powder out of Rubin's house. This powder, formulated from the substances Jordan learned about in California, was among the first shelf-stable probiotics to reach the market. Effectively creating the now wildly popular probiotics category, Jordan was selling about $2 million worth of the little bags per year.

One of the most extraordinary entrepreneurs I have ever known, Jordan is an exceptional storyteller who understands how to inspire people with his personal story, product, and purpose. He regained his health in spectacular fashion and made that story the centerpiece of his company's messaging. When I worked with him, he told his story repeatedly, honing it to its essence so he could recite it in an elevator or in front of five hundred people at a conference.

He didn't just want to sell a lot of products; he wanted to change lives.

You might say that his product and his purpose existed in perfect harmony. Here was someone living out my father's three maxims, boldly staking everything for his company, Garden of Life, and making a difference by helping others become healthier. Here was a project that aligned with everything I wanted in my own professional life.

And when I told Jordan this, he knew that inspiration and courage could only get him so far. He needed help scaling his company around a strategy, so he hired me to help him write a three-year business plan, which defined the path his little company would take to get to $15 million in annual revenue. He accomplished that goal three years later (almost to the day!). Then, he hired me as his CEO to work with him to draw up and execute a plan to attain the next three-year goal: $60 million in annual revenue.

Nestlé ended up acquiring the company for a boatload of money, and that little company is now helping millions of people around the globe. But none of this would have come to fruition had he not had a hugely personal, relatable story and a vision that kept his team rowing together and moving everything forward.

Today's entrepreneurs are still courageous, but—here's the rub—I'm not seeing many Jordans anymore. Today's entrepreneurs seem generally less bold about telling their personal stories and making their companies about something much bigger than their products or categories. And I have a theory as to why this is: the Squarespace(ification) of entrepreneurship. (Thanks to Emily Kanter of Cambridge Naturals for help putting a name on it!)

Leader Squarespacification

You are likely familiar with Squarespace, the website hosting service that offers templated websites that end up making brands practically indistinguishable from each other. The template pages contain product shots, logos, retailers, Order Now buttons, and testimonials—all different but basically the same.

Technology has lowered the barrier to innovation, which can be a good thing. But it has also dumbed us down a bit, which is not. I'm particularly dismayed by what has happened to the About Us tab, which is typically downplayed and sometimes hard to find. The opposite should be true: there's a fine line between letting your brand do the talking and allowing your voice and storytelling to shine through.

Another problem arises from boot camps and business incubators, such as Y Combinator, which tend to prioritize fast starts, rapid iteration of ideas, products, and services, and the growth and scalability of systems and operations. These are all important principles, to be sure, but what's missing is what Simon Sinek, the author of *Start with Why*, refers to as a "deeper purpose." The problem with keeping your deeper purpose out of the spotlight is that your brand is probably less distinctive than you are. For example, if your customer has three different probiotics to choose from, and only one of them promoted the story that it saved its leader's life, which one would stand out?

Have you ever considered the possibility that you might be more interesting than your product or service? If so, why hide yourself behind it?

The challenge, of course, is to find your story. This is not something you can just skip. I often use the storytelling techniques I learned from Bo Eason, an ex-NFL player turned Broadway star turned motivational speaker. He developed an exercise centered around four deep questions to ask yourself:

- **What are the 10 coolest things about me?** This is a time to drop the modesty and take pride in who you've become. Think about why you are cool and try to link it to a defining moment.

- **What captures my defining moment?** Dig deep to identify a moment or period that powerfully influenced your life.
- **What connects this moment to my business?** Ask how your defining moment led you to develop the superpowers needed to launch your company.
- **How can I tell this story?** Consider what it is about your company and yourself that should inspire others to trust your brand and buy your products.

Working your way through these questions in a logical, detailed fashion can help you overcome the tyranny of the online template and give customers, employees, investors, and other stakeholders a reason to be inspired and love your company.

A Personal Anthem

Steve Klinetobe, my colleague and inspiration catalyst at ScalePassion, is the guy business owners call to learn how to connect personal stories to brand strategy to business strategy, all to ensure that impact never gets squeezed out of the picture. Steve says every business owner should have a leader's anthem: a profound, emotionally charged testament to the *why* behind your entrepreneurial quest. "This anthem serves as a perpetual reminder, a passionate echo of your initial motivations, always within a hand's grasp, fueling your spirit," Steve explained. This is an essential initial step. Crafting your anthem early in your journey ensures authenticity and the raw passion needed to sustain you.

I once led a workshop for the Young Presidents' Organization (YPO) on personal storytelling. I worked with six CEOs to uncover their personal stories and then connect them to their companies. One of the CEOs,

Asheesh Advani, admitted to being teased and ridiculed as a boy because of a stutter. Asheesh founded CircleLending, a business that helped pioneer peer-to-peer lending between relatives, friends, and social network members. Today, he is CEO of JA Worldwide, a global NGO that provides hands-on educational programs and experiences related to entrepreneurship, work readiness, and financial literacy.

During the workshop, Asheesh traced his passion for developing confident and capable entrepreneurs directly to his own struggle to gain confidence as a stutterer. "What my speech therapist would do was give me a word like *buttons* and ask me to speak fluidly for a solid minute on the topic of buttons," recalled Asheesh. "Buttons aren't something most of us think much about, so I had to learn how to think ahead and form associations about buttons: buttons on my shirt, buttons on my pants, buttons that have been lost, or buttons that I've found lying on the sidewalk. I developed this skill for impromptu speaking that ended up helping me develop greater self-belief."

Helping other young people develop the confidence they need to assert themselves as leaders became his guiding passion and connection to the leaders he has met in his career. This great leader used his intense personal experience to build impact into his business. By the way, JA Worldwide was nominated for a 2024 Nobel Peace Prize.

Turn Your Passion into Your Purpose

You don't have to be operating at the level of Einstein or Michelangelo to turn your passion into your purpose, but you do have to discover what that passion—that thing you love to do and are good at—consists of.

The first way to learn is to realize that every human being on the planet has a zone of genius, or superpower. Your superpower isn't simply what you're good at—sales, marketing, operations, strategy, and so on—although superpowers are, by definition, things we excel at. They are also the thing we do with the least amount of prodding or self-inflicted torture. The thing we would do for free if we could. The thing others marvel at and say, "How do you *do* that?!" But above all, as we'll explore in the next chapter, your superpower is the activity that transports you into the *zone* where you draw limitless, self-replenishing energy that makes you feel glad to be alive.

As a general rule, business owners in the earliest stages of company growth wear multiple hats, although savvy leaders build their small start-up teams with versatile players. However, as the company grows into adolescence, business owners should aim to spend more than 50% to 75% of their time doing what they are naturally gifted at and, frankly, what no one else on their team can do. Everything else can and should be delegated.

But don't wait until you reach a specific size to move into your zone of genius. At my company, ScalePassion, my commitment to working in my zone of genius has attracted an awesome team that loves to do the other stuff.

A business owner's energy is anchored to living their purpose. If a leader's personal passion is the driving force of their organization's mission and vision, they stay energized and the energy becomes highly contagious. Stephen Covey's famous book *The 7 Habits of Highly Effective People* included the belief that "every person has a unique personal significance" that he called "finding your voice." Think about the things you find yourself talking about, thinking about, or reading about the most, and you'll know where your energy should be directed.

When you're working on naming your superpower, enlist some help. While nobody likes a braggart or someone who refuses to acknowledge imperfections, the truth is few of us want to say, even to ourselves, "I am *so great* at this!" or "This is my superpower!" Let others do that for you. One way to enlist others in discovering your superpower is a 360, which is short for 360 degrees of feedback. Some 360s elicit feedback from colleagues in the workforce. Others involve a wider network of people in your life, including colleagues, friends, fellow board members, professional organization members, and even family. When done correctly, a 360 can yield some incredibly sobering but encouraging insight into where you should focus your energy.

Here's an example of how a 360 works. We had a client that boasted a charismatic founder and a talented team, but they weren't clicking. In a typical 360, we gather the data, interview the team, and then deliver the tough message the CEO most needs to hear. In this case, we asked questions about the leader's strengths to leverage, weaknesses to delegate, opportunities for growth, and blind spots to manage. We synthesized the feedback and presented it to the client. The main takeaway from the 360 was that while the founder was viewed as an extremely creative, persuasive, and articulate champion of the brand—both within the company and with external audiences—he fell short on several important leadership traits, notably planning, setting and sticking to priorities, and "ownership," which related to being present with his team day-to-day.

The founder's expertise and passion for his mission also tended to make him seem arrogant, high-minded, and poor at listening, even though his team admired his collaborative nature, salesmanship, and sense of humor.

As a result of the 360, the client first hired a COO to delegate the planning, systems, and prioritization processes the team needed to do their work. Second, he pledged to devote more time to improving the product and its packaging, two action items that his team wanted to prioritize but hadn't been in the outwardly focused founder's mind. And, finally, freed from much of the day-to-day by his new COO, the founder determined to leverage his strong reputation in the industry and double down on his audience-facing communications, including a TED Talk and other thought-leadership activities.

A 360 isn't for the faint of heart, but the results can be absolutely game-changing.

Walking the Talk

Years ago, I hired a bright entrepreneur and doctor named Andrew Brandeis at MegaFood as our entrepreneur in residence. Later, when I started Findaway Adventures, my partners and I invested in his company, OK Capsule, which creates customized vitamin supplement packages for customers.

When we began working together, his staff was fairly miserable and it didn't take long to determine why this was the case. Andrew's superpower lies in creating a vision, developing products, and raising money. His team reported that his energy was high and very positive when he was doing these things. The problem was that Andrew also felt he needed to run the day-to-day, leading long, tactical meetings and slogging through the details that, while totally indispensable to the company's success, frankly bored Andrew to death. As a result, his energy during meetings suffered, and so did his team.

Andrew took the feedback to heart and handed off the day-to-day running to his COO, who absolutely loved making sure the sales, marketing, operations, and other trains ran on time.

Discovering your superpower is only the beginning; you also need to recognize and communicate how working in your superpower affects others. "I'm going to say no to that because that's not in my wheelhouse. This would be a great one to give to Paige," is the kind of language you need to become comfortable using to keep yourself and, ultimately, your team working in their superpowers to fulfill their purpose and the company's mission. But before anyone in your company can feel safe saying no to something that isn't in their wheelhouse, they need tacit permission from the CEO or founder, who sets the standard the other leaders and staff will follow.

Obviously, there is a limit to the amount of leeway you can give team members to say no to requests, but a company that has been built by a business owner who knows their purpose and has hired others to complement that purpose will likely be easier, not harder, to run.

Purpose Comes in All Sizes

When it comes to causes or purposes, size does not matter. Think of the business world as a human body for which every part—finger, elbow, eyelash, pancreas—serves a purpose. Each part of the body serves an important role that only it can serve as well as it does. The business world is the same way.

While a remarkable company like Patagonia may decide to make Earth its only shareholder and dedicate millions to environmental support, another company might focus on hiring employees who have served in the military or as first responders, and yet another might support other local business partnerships or school-to-work programs. The change-the-world movement is not dogmatic; every instance of doing something right strikes a little blow for a better world. If you doubt this, just remember what the Dalai Lama has said about making an impact: "If you think you're too small to make a difference, try sleeping with a mosquito."

Take a Little Test

As the leader goes, so goes the business, right? Get your mind in the right space by figuring out your purpose and your zone of genius and directing them toward creating a more impactful (and rewarding) life. Here are several tools to get you started and that you can then refer to at every stage of scaling impact:

1. Answer these five questions in no more than two sentences each:
   a. What is my purpose / personal mission?
   b. When am I most in my zone of genius?
   c. What energizes me the most?
   d. What energizes me the least?
   e. How can I express my personal mission through my business?
2. Check out the companion material from the *Nail Your Strategy* journal, which my team and I put together to guide impact-minded business owners through the key touch points of scaling impact. Download it here: www.scalepassion.com/nail-your-strategy-journal.
3. Take a short online leadership assessment to help see where you stand in your impact journey. Access it here: www.changetheworldleader.com.

Lew's Tips & Resources

Are you ready to harness that power that comes from tapping into your superpower of purpose? Are you bold enough to take this first step? To stand out in the crowd? To tell your very personal story as a way of calling people into your movement?

Maxim 1: Make a Difference

- **Pursue purpose beyond passion:** Distinguish between passion and purpose, where purpose involves a desire for change. Discover your larger purpose through introspection and alignment with the difference you want to make.
- **Develop your personal leader's anthem:** Craft a profound leader's anthem and personal story to inspire others and align your business with a deeper purpose.
- **Tap into the power of personal storytelling:** Use storytelling techniques to connect with your audience and communicate your mission effectively.

Maxim 2: Be Bold

- **Be authentic:** Boldly share your personal story and vision to inspire others and drive your company forward. Embrace authenticity by letting your voice and storytelling shine through, rather than conforming to generic business templates.
- **Turn your passion into your purpose:** Identify your zone of genius or superpower–the activity that brings you limitless energy and fulfillment. Focus on spending the majority of your time in this zone as your company grows.

Maxim 3: Do It Right

- **Reflect and take action:** Reflect on your purpose, zone of genius, and what energizes you the most and least. Consider how you can express your personal mission through your business, and utilize resources to guide your journey.
- **Understand that purpose comes in all sizes:** Remember that purpose can manifest in various forms, from supporting environmental causes to hiring employees who have faced barriers to employment. Embrace the opportunity to make a difference, no matter the scale.

Books or Articles to Consider

- *The Purpose Driven Life* by Rick Warren
- *Start with Why* by Simon Sinek
- *The Alchemist* by Paulo Coelho

Scale Passion Resources

- "Are You Ready to Scale Your Personal Leadership?" assessment: map your opportunities for harnessing your purpose
- "Find Your Personal Purpose" worksheet: a simple guide for going deeper on purpose exploration
- Exponential Purpose Workshop: a guided approach to connecting your personal purpose to your corporate one
- "Leadership 360" exercise: a guided approach to gaining stakeholder input on your leadership
- "Finding Your Zone of Genius" exercises: a do-it-yourself approach to defining your zone of genius

Find a comprehensive list of resources at ScalePassion.com/Resources.

Chapter 3

Superpower #2: Your Energy

Jeff Byers has rarely suffered from low energy. Growing up in Colorado, he was what you would call an active child who was always involved in sports. He played football at the University of Southern California (USC) and won a national championship with the Trojans in 2004. Jeff was a true student athlete who managed to captain his USC team while earning an MBA. He went on to the NFL, where he played for the Seattle Seahawks, Denver Broncos, and Carolina Panthers over the course of four years.

After leaving professional football in 2014, Jeff sought a finance career but quickly realized that it did not fulfill his deeper need to create something himself. So, he and a cofounder acquired the rights to a product he personally loved, PR Lotion, and built the brand known today as Momentous: a wellness company committed to finding health solutions for high performers of all calibers.

Jeff works with distinguished doctors, scientists, athletes, military personnel, and nearly two hundred professional and collegiate sports organizations across the country. His purpose is to "democratize high performance" by educating consumers who, said Jeff, "can become overwhelmed by getting advice from people who aren't providing them with information that is best suited for them, their lifestyle, or their individual wellness goals."

When ScalePassion started working with Jeff, his cofounder Erica Good, and his team, one of our exercises used Patrick Lencioni's Working Genius tool, which allows you to determine your zone of genius, zone of frustration, and the zone in between those two extremes. After using the tool, Jeff emerged as a galvanizer, someone who rallies the troops. We recognized this trait immediately in Jeff and nicknamed this persona inside him Big G. There was a prominent place for a Big G in a fast-growing company competing in a saturated marketplace, but leading daily meetings was, perhaps, not the right place. Jeff was an elite athlete, but he saw himself as an educator and advocate and needed to align his energy around what he could accomplish in that role, which was to galvanize passion and action—much like an NFL linebacker might motivate his teammates on the field.

When he showed up at meetings with his Big G persona and started radiating energy and dominating the conversation, he stopped listening to his team. And they stopped trying to talk. After working with us to identify and better manage his Big G persona, Jeff learned how to harness his energy and become much more aware of when he was using it and its impact on his team.

Your Sweet Spot

The way to ensure that your energy remains robust is to operate in your sweet spot—being on purpose, utilizing your zone of genius, and generally staying in your commitment.

Here's an example from my own career. Several years into my tenure as CEO at MegaFood, we made the decision to pivot from a retail-centric model to omnichannel—putting the consumer in the middle of our universe over the retailer. With the rise in direct-to-consumer marketing made possible by e-commerce and the increasing scope of Amazon, we needed to put the consumer in the center of everything we did. And we needed to pivot fast. So, I came up with the idea of doing a company-wide meeting, a town hall, around the theme of summiting Mount Everest. My role would be to stand up on the stage and articulate the need for the pivot and rally a couple of hundred employees around the arduous task of reaching the summit—all to inspire this big pivot for our company.

Fulfilling my role was easy. Articulating a vision and laying it out before my team is something I love to do, and it energizes me to go to any length needed to succeed. What did not energize me was planning the particulars of the town hall. Part of the art of persuasion and advocacy is to turn a boring meeting into an exciting and memorable event. For that, I turned to my vision activator, who happened to be Ashley, my executive assistant and chief of staff at the time. I said, "Here's your budget. Have at it!" She nailed all the details, which included fake snow, hundreds of fleece snowballs, and an oxygen bar. The different departments tended to sit at the same table, so occasionally, little snowball fights would break out between sales and marketing or regulatory and operations teams.

We'll go deeper into this event in chapter 13, but—spoiler alert—we successfully made the pivot in about 12 months. I am sure you also noted another takeaway: while I was in my sweet spot around inspiring, Ashley was in hers, turning vision into reality by creating meaningful and memorable events.

Plug the Leaks

There are numerous ways we leak energy. Operating outside your sweet spot is a major one.

Do you remember Andrew from the previous chapter? Andrew is an entrepreneur, but he sees himself, first and foremost, as a doctor. In this persona, he sees himself as someone who understands how his new formulas and personalized packages of supplements support people wishing to live healthier lives. When he's sharing this knowledge in front of customers and investors, he feels he's doing—as well as anyone ever did—what he was put on Earth to do.

But when he has to sit at a big conference room table and energize a room full of team members about the details of running a business, his energy plummets. It's hard to lead a group of employees in routine meetings. You have to be present, establish a cadence for the conversation, and show empathy, compassion, and helpfulness around the problems that arise in marketing, operations, and the like. When doing something causes you dread or seems to kill your soul a little bit, pay attention because the pain you're feeling just might be the crack through which your energy is leaking.

Plug it up. One way or another, plug up the leak and reboot your power source. Here are three ideas for plugging those leaks:

1. Find someone else who gains energy doing the thing that drains yours, and delegate with clarity.
2. Organize the energy-draining event right when you come off an event where your energy is the highest.
3. When all else fails, confront your low energy, and ask for ideas or help from team members—you will be blown away when someone always steps in to support!

Supercharge Your Daily Routine

Maintaining high levels of resonant energy requires thoughtful management of daily habits that go beyond your actual work. Business owners have to prioritize self-care and well-being to sustain their vitality and avoid burnout.

The healthiest business owners diligently manage their energy by designing their daily routines and habits in detail. One trick involves setting up gateway habits that serve as prompts for productive activities during the day. For example, setting out your workout outfit and shoes before you go to bed at night makes it far more likely that you'll put them on and run in them the next morning. If you are committed to eating clean and enjoy starting the day with a smoothie, then prep all your fruits and veggies for the week on Sunday and portion them out for daily use.

I worked with a business owner who lives in California, and one day he showed up for a meeting with very low energy. When I asked him how he was feeling, he said he felt stressed and overwhelmed, which absolutely killed his energy switch.

"What brings you energy?" I asked him. "Think of the last time you felt really great energy: What were you doing?"

"I don't know," he began. And then his eyes lit up big. "A couple of months ago, I was really into surfing. I love to surf."

"Okay, you haven't surfed in a while. Go surfing tomorrow!"

And he said, "Yeah, well. I don't have time for surfing."

"No, dude, you're not getting it," I replied. "You need this daily driver to restore your energy. *You need to surf.* Low energy for you means low energy for the company."

Jeff Byers may have traded in his shoulder pads for a laptop, but he recognizes that he draws his energy from physical activity. He starts his day by throwing on a weighted backpack and rucking around the neighborhood. All of us have, or can cultivate, these cornerstone activities that center us and energize us for the tasks ahead. These activities can include exercise, meditation, or completing little tasks that would otherwise draw down our energy by distracting us. These cornerstone activities give us a sense of accomplishment that sends a healthy shot of dopamine coursing through our bodies.

The stress-busting benefits of dopamine are so well documented that they seem cliché, but we'll repeat them anyway. They improve decision-making and cognitive function. A 2014 study called "Mindful-ness Training and Stress Resilience" published in the journal *Psychological Science* found that mindfulness meditation training led to improvements in decision-making and reduced susceptibility to sunk-cost bias, a com-mon cognitive bias in decision-making in which we continue to do the wrong thing because we feel we've invested too much in it already. Is it just me or does this sound like a variation on Albert Einstein's famous defini-tion of insanity—doing the same thing over and over again and expecting different results?

Chronic stress is associated with a range of negative health outcomes, including cardiovascular disease, hypertension, and mental health disor-ders. Any way you can find to reduce stress will help both you and col-leagues enjoy healthier, more productive lives. A 2014 study called "Do Workplace Health Promotion (Wellness) Programs Work?" published in the *Journal of Occupational and Environmental Medicine* has shown that stress management programs, including relaxation techniques and cog-nitive-behavioral interventions, can result in increased productivity, re-duced absenteeism, and improved job satisfaction among employees.

Who wouldn't want *all* those things?

In his book *Energy Leadership*, Bruce Schneider argues that leaders need to keep not one but four dimensions of energy in alignment. There is emotional energy that is deeply connected to our relationships both at work and outside work, spiritual energy that comes from working and living within our purpose and in accordance with our values, and physical and mental energy that come from staying fit in mind and body through exercise, reading, podcasts, professional development, or any of the 10 thousand other ways to replenish resources and rewire circuitry.

Most importantly, argues Schneider, the more energy we have across the board, the more present we can be and the less likely we are to become combative, resentful, or frustrated. Leadership is like a chair with the four legs of physical, mental, emotional, and spiritual energy. As you commit to proactively supporting these legs, you will witness the transformative power they hold.

Quiet Time Replenishes

When I was the CEO at MegaFood, the only time I closed my office door was to meditate, which I did, and continue to do, every day. One of the biggest misconceptions about meditation is that it's all about "quiet" and blocking out the world around you. The opposite is probably closer to the mark: meditation puts you in closer touch with your surroundings and with yourself. Meditation seeks mindfulness and a state of being aware of everything that comes into your consciousness, but doing so in a way that doesn't judge or distort this input to fit whatever dramas are in or have dominated your life.

I want to spend just a bit of time on meditation and what meditation circles call the sacred pause.

I got into meditation after listening to one of my favorite podcasts, *The Tim Ferriss Show,* during which Tim Ferriss interviews people from all walks of life who share one thing in common: they're exceptionally good at something. His conversations with them seek to deconstruct what makes them tick. I've followed Ferriss long enough to conclude that one of the most common practices among his many guests is meditation.

This was an important learning for me as a leader. And back in 2012, I began meditating with help from an app called Headspace. Another great one is Sam Harris's Waking Up app. Both offer introductory courses that teach you how to exercise your mind in a new way, like learning to flex a new muscle. For me, 20 minutes each day has come to feel about right. Meditation helps me understand why I'm feeling the way I am and put space between a stimulus and response before deciding what to do with it. This process is known as the sacred pause. It is completely transforming me as a CEO and a person.

Even though you may practice meditation for only a short time each day, the practice carries forward into the rest of the day, allowing you to recognize the things that really get you riled up and red faced. For example, I get riled by being ignored or misunderstood, having constraints or excuses thrown up as roadblocks to progress, and getting mired in the minutiae of detailed work. Meditation helps me separate fact from story (a critical leadership skill we'll go deeper into in stage 2) and become a much better listener to others' points of view, since I won't find these threatening and thus can be more present in the conversation.

I'm not saying you can't be present without it, but meditation makes it much easier to avoid viewing interactions as win or lose or zero-sum games. This habit of mind reduces my fears, and fear is a huge devourer of energy. Fear is also a major underlying factor in stress, which is a symptom of fear. So, to all the other pillars of energy we've discussed in this chapter, I would add meditation as a key component of happiness. And if you still need more proof about the efficacious outcomes of meditation, I refer you to a 2021 article called "Relationships Between Mindfulness, Purpose in Life, Happiness, Anxiety, and Depression: Testing a Mediation Model in a Sample of Women," published in the *International Journal of Environmental Research and Public Health*. The authors concluded, "Mindfulness is associated with both a sense of purpose in life and engagement in activities, which are also connected with positive outcomes."

As we'll see in stage 2, you can scale energy within your organization to great effect, but as usual, it all starts with the leader's energy. And the closer you look at this remarkable resource called energy, the more you see that *focus* is a key driver.

Lew's Tips & Resources

My dad worked for the airlines, and this reminds me of a commonly heard phrase before takeoff: "Put your own oxygen mask on before assisting others." This really speaks to the essence of energy. As the founder or leader goes, so goes the business. You cannot boldly make a difference in the world if you are stressed and exhausted all the time! So, do it right, and get your energy straight.

Maxim 1: Make a Difference

- **Identify your sweet spot:** Operating within your sweet spot ensures that your energy remains robust. This involves being on purpose, utilizing your zone of genius, and staying committed to your goals.
- **Plug the leaks:** Recognize activities that drain your energy and address them promptly. Operating outside your sweet spot can lead to leaks in energy. Pay attention to tasks that cause you dread or make you feel disconnected from your purpose.
- **Supercharge your daily routine:** Prioritize self-care and well-being to sustain your vitality and avoid burnout. Design daily routines that include activities such as exercise, meditation, or completing tasks that energize you.

Maxim 2: Be Bold

- **Harness your energy:** Learn to harness your energy effectively by being aware of how you use it, when you use it, and how it impacts your team.
- **Delegate effectively:** Recognize your strengths and weaknesses, and delegate tasks that drain your energy to others who excel in those areas. For example, delegate event planning details to

someone who enjoys and excels at organizing events, allowing you to focus on your strengths.

Maxim 3: Do It Right

- **Prioritize gateway habits:** Implement gateway habits that serve as prompts for productive activities during the day. For example, prepping workout clothes the night before makes it more likely that you'll exercise in the morning.
- **Embrace meditation:** Incorporate meditation into your daily routine to enhance mindfulness, improve decision-making, and reduce stress. Meditation helps you separate fact from story and become a better listener, ultimately contributing to your overall well-being and leadership effectiveness.

Books or Articles to Consider

- *The 6 Types of Working Genius* by Patrick Lencioni
- *Atomic Habits* by James Clear
- *Energy Leadership* by Bruce Schneider

Tools to Consider

- Headspace meditation app (headspace.com)
- Waking Up meditation app (wakingup.com)
- Working Genius tool (workinggenius.com)
- MyFitnessPal nutrition and health tracker (myfitnesspal.com)

Scale Passion Resources

- "Are You Ready to Scale Your Personal Leadership?" assessment: map your opportunities for harnessing your purpose

Find a comprehensive list of resources at ScalePassion.com/Resources.

Chapter 4

Superpower #3: Your Focus

'𝗏e been listening to *The Andy Stanley Leadership Podcast* for years. Andy Stanley is humble and insightful and offers lots of helpful ways of thinking about leadership. One of his memorable discussions, which he titled "Doing What Only You Can Do," involved delegation.

As I listened, I found myself nodding in agreement when he said (and I'm paraphrasing here), the two best secrets are that the less you do, the more you accomplish, and the less you do, the more you let others accomplish better than you could.

His larger point was that business owners often have trouble getting out of their own way. Maybe they think they have to set the tone for their organization and do everything. Maybe they think they have something to prove to show their team why they should be trusted. Or, just as likely, they think they're the smartest person in the room and must always, always set every agenda. The problem with these patterns, Stanley said, was that good or even great leaders often aren't good at everything. Their team knows this, or quickly learns it, and tries to wrest away the things the leader can't do well. Struggles and misunderstandings can ensue, and that's not good for anybody.

In other words, summed up Stanley—and this is a phrase I love—"well-roundedness is overrated." The moment the leader steps away from his core competencies, his performance suffers. Especially if he interferes with others who are working in their core competencies and have to entertain his bad ideas!

This chapter offers you an outline of how to start making yourself better focused than you've ever been in your life. It looks at not only goal setting but also building in accountability—to yourself, your family, your colleagues—and bolstering that accountability on a yearly, monthly, weekly, and even daily basis by developing the habits you need to move toward your goals. The key is to clear away the clutter on your desk and your inbox as well as between your ears. Focus is a gift you deserve to give yourself—no, a gift you *have* to give yourself if you want to be bold and make a difference.

Holiday Reflection

For the past decade, I have taken two weeks off around Christmas and New Year's to reflect on the past year and plan for the coming one. My inspiration came from author and podcaster Tim Ferriss, who wrote a blog recommending that we focus on reviewing the past year rather than making resolutions for the next year. My past year review involves going through my calendar and evaluating all the things I've done in terms of whether they got my energy up or down. Then I use this data to plan the next year in a way that energizes me the most.

For example, one year my reflection resulted in my determination to become certified as a conscious leadership coach and begin working toward that goal in the coming year. This year, my objectives included writing a book and preparing for more public speaking. I have also decided to dive deeper into the conscious capitalism community, whose philosophy of providing value for all stakeholders complements my own views of scaling impact.

I see this as the first step in harnessing my focus. Taking a macro view of my life, reconnecting with my purpose, and getting very intentional about what I want in the coming months or year.

Drivers

To stay in your best energy, you want to break down this longer-term planning and yearly goal setting into monthly, weekly, and daily drivers. A driver is an activity or habit that brings me closer to achieving a goal. For example, if one of my long-term goals is to keep my weight within an optimal range, I set up a monthly driver tracking my body-fat percentage. One of my goals is to maintain a healthy social life with my wife, so we set up weekly date nights to make sure this happens. I track how much free time, prep time, and client-facing work time (the drivers) I spend on ScalePassion to keep me moving toward my goal of having each of these areas take up an equal third of my time.

My weekly and daily drivers have to do with meditation, which I want to do at least five times a week, along with eating clean six days a week and working out at least four times a week. I track these daily drivers when I review my personal flight plan (see page 81).

Seize the Day

One way to drive focus specifically for today is something I call a rolling start. It's a daily ritual I use to keep myself on track and clearheaded. Here's what I do:

1. Adjust my standing desk to the right height and take a big, deep breath.
2. Clear my email inbox down to zero. Yes, I am one of those crazy folks that commits to inbox zero. I just can't handle the pressure that

comes from having email overload. If an email requires some action on my part, I forward it to Asana, my preferred project- and task-management tool. If not, I note it and delete it. For e-newsletters and emails from brands I like to buy, I use an app called Unroll.Me that serves up one email a day with all the things I want to read and leaves out the rest, which clutters my inbox and my mind.

3. Review my personal flight plan (for more on this, see chapter 5). I take literally two minutes to run through my purpose, core values, goals, aspirations, and critical success factors—i.e., what I want to accomplish—for the day, week, and beyond in my personal life. My personal flight plan helps to give me a broader, longer view before I dive into the tactical, here-and-now activities.

4. Review my ScalePassion flight plan. Then I turn to my business and do the same exercise by reviewing the purpose, goals, and aspirations for the company, focusing on what's most important right now so I get a clear picture of our priorities (for more on this, see stage 2). Note: steps three and four might take only a couple of minutes each day, but they are critical moments of reflection and commitment and are core to prioritization. You will be surprised how quickly your personal and corporate flight plans become ingrained—but don't ever skip this step. Think of it as the critical path to focus.

5. Organize my commitments with a project-management tool. Having established my goals and priorities, I plan out my week using Asana, acting on the emails that required me to act and prioritizing my goals and aspirations with actual delivery times. I block off key times in my week for bigger projects and move tasks to the appropriate day in Asana so that I do not see them until that day.

6. Meditate. This is my cornerstone habit. I used to do this first but found myself distracted by all the things that needed to be done. So, having done my housekeeping and putting things in their proper place, I can now enjoy greater mindfulness for the 15 to 20

minutes I meditate. My favorite meditation app is Waking Up, but if you are a beginner, Headspace is a great place to start.

7. Get stuff done (GSD). Now that I have everything lined up and my head is in a good place, free of fear and anxiety, I'm ready to start getting stuff done.

I find that I can get this whole ritual done in maybe 15 to 30 minutes, except for meditation, which adds a bit more time that's well worth it. I try to do some version of this routine every day, and I appreciate having recourse to it when I feel distracted or overwhelmed.

Establish a Weekly Rhythm of Accountability

The best business owners I know invariably have a leadership coach who, among other duties, helps keep them accountable to themselves and their organizations. The research backs up my anecdotal experience. Research published in a 2007 article called "The Impact of Commitment, Accountability, and Written Goals on Goal Achievement," in the journal *Dominican Scholar*, looked at 267 participants recruited from businesses, organizations, and business networking groups. The findings showed conclusively that participants who wrote down their intentional goals and shared them achieved far greater success—7.6 out of 8 mean goal achievement—than those with unwritten, unintentional, and unshared goals, whose mean goal achievement was 4.28/8.

My first and current leadership coach, Nick Van Nice, and I check in biweekly to review my progress against the personal and professional goals I have and whether my purpose, energy, and focus are in sync. Often enough, they are not; one of the great services an ace coach provides is an outlet for unproductive emotions. For example, one of my triggers is when I feel someone isn't listening to me, which I interpret as a sign of disrespect. Now, even if my observation is correct and they're not listening, snapping at them or stewing privately doesn't help either of us, right? So, instead of getting triggered in front of that employee and, for example, firing them on the spot, a good coach helps me process that emotion so I handle the situation more productively.

Finally, a good coach helps you traverse the journey from A, the kind of leader you are now, to Z, the kind of leader you want to become. I call this ABZ coaching, with *B* designating the immediate next steps—reading books; attending conferences, trainings, and workshops; networking; meditating; and more—you need to take to make the journey.

Coaches can also help you think more deeply about work-family or work–personal life balance. Too many of us are quick to settle for having to choose between them rather than making both work. I see work life and personal life as interwoven, and I think it only fair that both are factored into my plans and daily priorities. Most of us are multifaceted people who have commitments to family, friends, colleagues, employees, you name it. Where many people slip up is in losing sight of what is most important right now. I'm not exaggerating when I say that how you will balance your work and your personal life is a question you need to ask yourself every day—and you need to answer it as it pertains to not only work but also your family, health, leisure, spirituality, and so forth.

Prioritize your personal roles. Take care of yourself and your family. Go through the exercise of force ranking all the roles you play—spouse, parent, colleague, leader, tennis partner—and then decide what is most important right now for each role.

Making It Conscious

If you've meditated at all, you know that one of the ends of this practice is mindfulness, which means making the unconscious *conscious*. We seek to become more aware so that we can become more intentional about what we do and what we focus on. What we focus on will depend on the roles, or personas, we have taken on as colleague, boss, spouse, parent, club member, volunteer, and so on. And then based upon your vision for yourself in each of these roles, you identify what is most important for you to focus on today, this week, this year, five years from now, and 25 years from now.

Yes, you will have to make choices, but not the kind of choices you think you have to make. For example, can you realistically build a billion-dollar company from scratch and coach all three of your kids' soccer, basketball, and baseball teams from the time they are six until they reach junior high school? Very unlikely. But your choice isn't *between* being a successful entrepreneur or business leader and being a present and nurturing parent. Your choice is whether you honor the commitments you make in your role as an entrepreneur and parent.

Are you making conscious choices about what gets done and what doesn't? Are you surrounding yourself with people—e.g., a partner, colleagues, investors, friends—who complement and support the priorities you have set for your work and life?

These are not questions you learn to answer in business school. I know this because I've been to business school. A business school talks about building a business plan that has nothing to do with the leader's passion or purpose or the multiple commitments in the various roles they will inhabit in life. Yet, the positive energy you receive by identifying and then focusing on these commitments is precisely what allows you to sidestep the pitfalls of burnout and disillusionment that plague many leaders and entrepreneurs.

Your lack of consciously outlining and communicating your current focus and priorities leads to the energy leaks we discussed in chapter 3. Leaks that often lead to disillusionment and burnout.

And remember: as the leader goes, so goes the business. When you are focused and acting with great intentionality, your team will follow suit and be more engaged in your company's mission and purpose. Or to bring it closer to earth, when your typical workday and your typical week energize you and motivate you to add value because you are focused on what matters most right now, your team will be far more likely to feel and behave the same.

Lead on Focus

Years ago, at a YPO Forum that met monthly, I was whining about my hectic workweek to my fellow young presidents, telling them how I couldn't keep up with my calendar. One of my peers smiled and said, "You know, Rob, you're the f*ckin' CEO, right? Make the schedule that works for you and your team will follow."

Lesson learned. After that, I went on to become far more intentional about the way I planned my weeks, with special attention to concentrating on certain areas on certain days. For example, currently my ideal week looks like the following calendar.

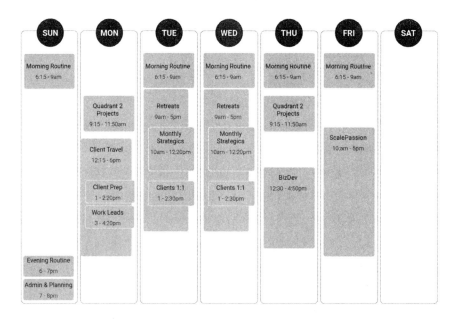

Everyone's workweek looks different, but you can still use your calendar to say no to distractions that cut into your proactive plan, freeing you to focus, focus, and focus. What's more, by planning out your workweek in this way, you can get yourself in the right frame of mind for different tasks. You need to be in a different mindset when you're doing business development than you do when coaching a client or holding meetings with your team. Business owners are wearers of many hats but shouldn't insist on wearing them all at the same time. Eventually, you can cascade your well-planned week out to your leaders who will follow your lead and structure their meetings and projects for optimal focus. But we'll get to that later.

Only Do What Only You Can Do

Before you can delegate with clarity and purpose as a leader of others, you need to be able to determine what only you should focus on. Focus is one of the hardest things to achieve as a business owner who feels the need to wear many hats. That's why, as a coach, I'm fond of what has become known as the 80/20 rule, or the Pareto principle, named after the Italian economist Vilfredo Pareto. One interpretation of the principle is that most of your productivity or results, around 80%, come from a relatively small but focused effort—around 20%—you put into something. It stands to reason that the sooner you can get yourself doing whatever it is that constitutes that 20% of high-productivity effort, the better.

A related principle that applies to focus is the law of diffusion, which says that because you only have so much time, you have to prioritize the things that matter the most. I know a client hasn't mastered the art of focus when they have several big goals they're working on at the same time. My advice is almost always to ask them to decide what's most important and get uber focused on it; otherwise, the law of diffusion kicks in.

One way to think about diffusion is to consider the difference between the sun beaming through a pane of glass and the sun going through a magnifying lens. The former lights up a room; the latter, because the rays are focused on a single point, can literally create a laser that can cut through steel! Do you remember Momentous? Once we knew that Erica was the strategist and manager and Jeff the visionary and galvanizer, we went so far as to break down who made what kind of decisions. Now that is doing what only Erica or Jeff can do.

Lew's Tips & Resources

When Dad said "do it right," I am certain that "it" really mattered in this maxim. Knowing the right "it" means prioritization and focus. Only through focus will you maximize your personal impact.

Maxim 1: Make a Difference

- **Delegate wisely:** Recognize that the less you do, the more you can accomplish and empower others to excel in areas where they have core competencies. Avoid interfering in tasks where you lack expertise, as this can hinder overall performance.
- **Reflect and plan:** Take time for reflection and planning, such as during the holidays, to evaluate past achievements and set meaningful goals for the future. Focus on activities that energize you and align with your purpose, both personally and professionally.

Maxim 2: Be Bold

- **Master the art of focus:** Embrace the 80/20 rule, also known as the Pareto principle, to identify the most productive tasks that only you can accomplish. Avoid spreading yourself too thin by prioritizing activities that contribute the most to your goals and leveraging the law of diffusion to maintain focus.
- **Prioritize accountability:** Engage with a leadership coach or accountability partner to stay focused on your goals and effectively navigate challenges. Regular check-ins can help you process emotions, maintain alignment with your purpose, and make conscious choices about your priorities.

Maxim 3: Do It Right

- **Establish daily rituals:** Create a daily ritual, like a rolling start, to keep yourself on track and clearheaded. Incorporate habits such as inbox management, reviewing personal and business flight plans, meditation, and organizing commitments to set the tone for a focused and productive day.
- **Structure your week:** Plan your week intentionally, allocating time for different tasks and maintaining a balance between proactive planning and getting stuff done (GSD). Cascade your well-structured week to your team to promote optimal focus and productivity throughout the organization.

Further Listening and Reading

- *The Andy Stanley Leadership Podcast*
- *The 7 Habits of Highly Effective People* by Stephen Covey
- "Impeccable Agreements" handout by Conscious Leadership Group (conscious.is)

Tools to Consider

- Asana: personal task and project management (asana.com)
- Trello: personal task and project management (trello.com)

Scale Passion Resources

- "Finding Your Zone of Genius" exercises: a do-it-yourself approach to defining your zone of genius
- *Your Personal Flight Plan* workbook: a do-it-yourself guide for harnessing your personal purpose
- "The Green Sheet Delegation Approach": a guide for teaching delegation across your organization

Find a comprehensive list of resources at ScalePassion.com/Resources.

Chapter 5

Superpower #4: Your Mindset

When I was hired by a private equity company to run MegaFood, I had already been a three-time CEO at consumer-packaged goods (CPG) companies, and the private equity (PE) firm had never done CPG before. I did not agree completely with the PE firm, who I believed were far too focused on maximizing earnings before interest, taxes, depreciation, and amortization (EBITDA) too early in the company's growth.

My view was that it takes money to make money, so I wanted the PE firm to invest more in marketing to grow the top line. They wanted me to do more with less. I chalked this up to typical PE greed. I began to think of myself as a victim and was constantly upset. And my upset trickled down to my leadership team and to the edges of the company. We continued to grow, but slowly and with much more drama—for which I was largely responsible.

I learned about conscious leadership through YPO and began working with Jim Fallon, an ex-founder and CEO and new conscious leadership coach, who taught me to take 100% responsibility for my thoughts and feelings. As I did that, I saw myself less as a misunderstood victim and more as someone being given an opportunity to learn something new. The whole world began to seem like an ally rather than an adversary. I was able to grow close with the board and see they did have my best interests at heart.

And we started doing more with less and getting more creative with our resources. I stretched my abilities and became a better CEO and more valuable to the board. We sold the company for one of the largest multiples the industry had ever seen at the time. My chief recollection of the shift was how smoothly everything went after this—for me and my team, who picked up on the new energy boost I got from my new mindset.

That's what getting your mindset right can do for you.

If a leader is happy and enlivened and motivated, so will the business be. If the leader is grumpy and pissed off all the time, so will the business be. If a leader shows emotional intelligence, follows through on agreements he makes with others, takes 100% responsibility for how they feel and think about something, acknowledges those feelings and thoughts to others, and communicates clearly with others, so will the business. These attributes describe a mindset of integrity that the business owner models for the entire organization.

As Stephen Covey explains in *The 7 Habits of Highly Effective People*, mindset is a fundamental way of seeing and acting in the world. Covey distinguishes the "abundance mindset" from the "scarcity mindset." The former posits that we live in a win-win world with plenty of everything for everybody, and that we have the agency to achieve the things we want if we put the effort toward achieving it. The scarcity mindset posits the reverse: life is a zero-sum game replete with winners and losers; it's also just as likely to bite us in the butt as it is to reward us for our efforts.

Allow me to come right out and say that if you wish to be a change-the-world leader, you have to adopt an abundance mindset. There are few things about which we will be dogmatic in this book, but this is one of them. Businesses are supposed to be built to grow, but how can you expect to enlist the help of others to grow your business and scale your passion if you don't believe in growing yourself, personally? Can't be done.

And why is mindset so important? Mindset is the whole enchilada. It's the combination of your purpose, energy, and focus all working together and spiraling upward to create the leader you show to yourself and the world. In this chapter, you'll learn how values like awareness and personal responsibility can empower you to live a life of integrity, the necessary first step in inspiring others to do the same.

Take Responsibility

Your success flows from your mindset as surely as water from a mountain stream flows downhill. If you are leading a $3 million company that can't seem to grow any more, then you are 100% committed to that company staying at $3 million—in other words, you are responsible for where you are. If you understand why this is so, you are on the way to achieving an abundance mindset. Remember, an abundance mindset does not mean that you think you have everything you want or need; it means you believe you have agency in what happens in your life.

Fear furnishes the main roadblock to enjoying the fruits of an abundant mindset. Emotions are a big part of life (and leadership). We're born hardwired to feel a range of emotions—joy, sadness, fear, anger, inspiration—and our life experiences create more complex emotions such as guilt, jealousy, boredom, and annoyance. Our emotions can protect or delight us, but they can also make us do or say things we regret—almost as soon as we say or do them.

The most important thing to understand about emotions: They are not good or bad. They simply are. They serve as important support for your superpowers—but only if you learn to embrace and interpret them. Even the emotions we've come to regard as "negative," such as fear and anger, serve an important evolutionary purpose. Seated in our amygdala, the part of the brain that controls emotions and our fight or flight response, emotions attempt to protect us from danger. This is why rather than trying to suppress or deny emotions, you should feel them as fully as you can so you can understand the source and the best way to respond.

For example, the emotion of anger tells us that something needs to stop. The emotion of fear means something needs to be faced. Often, those things that make us angry or fearful—such as, for instance, my tendency to feel angry when I feel a person isn't listening to me—can be overcome rationally and constructively. If I can feel anger coming on and understand why it is, I can turn my unconscious feelings into conscious understanding almost at the snap of my fingers. I couldn't always do this, of course, but practicing conscious leadership has given me some mental space to casually ask my (non)listener, "Are you with me?" rather than allow my anger to build.

Leading a dynamic organization requires passion *and* circumspection. I have passion in spades, so I've been practicing the calm needed to balance it. When I took up meditation as part of my larger commitment to conscious leadership, I learned about the emotional impacts of triggers and fuels. Fuels are things that feed your energy and focus. For me, this might be teaching something, brainstorming with someone, or breaking bread with a friend. Triggers are things that suck the energy out of you or drag you down and make it hard to focus. For me, this includes things that signal disrespect, such as eye-rolling at meetings, or things that suggest there is "no way out," such as getting mired in endless details.

Leaders are constantly being triggered and constantly being fueled. There's no way around it, but what matters is whether you're conscious of being triggered or fueled. How do you know? The Conscious Leadership Group has delineated "above the line" and "below the line" thinking. When we're operating below the line, we feel that life is happening *to us*; we may be a victim, villain, or hero, but in each case, we're feeling reactive and embattled. When we're operating above the line, we feel life is happening *by us*. We have agency. In fact, we have more than agency: we have 100% responsibility for our situation.

Awareness Is Crucial

Are you thinking that being above the line complements an abundance mindset? If so, you've absolutely nailed the mindset: 100% responsibility equals personal agency. I urge you to get curious about the things that make you tick or tick you off. What are your blind spots?

One way I was able to gain greater insight into my mental and emotional habits simply involved conducting my own little 360 review and asking friends and colleagues to point out the good, bad, and ugly in my behavior that I would never have identified on my own. I picked the consensus top five triggers and top five fuels and wrote them down for daily reference. Doing so makes me more generally aware because I can use my list to remind myself of upcoming situations that may test me. And no matter how busy I think I am, I can go out of my way to put myself in fuel-friendly places to recharge my batteries.

Another tool I've used is the Siberian North Railroad, an acronym (SBNRR) for how to respond to triggers and emotional hot spots. The acronym stands for stop, breathe, notice, reflect, and respond. Hey, if it's good enough for Google, which made headlines using the practice in a 2012 *New York Times* article called "OK, Google, Take a Deep Breath," it might be worth trying on your campus.

Earlier we talked about meditation and the sacred pause, a patient, watchful, calm moment during which you check your head, heart, and gut for the way to proceed. Once you've attained this mental state, whatever rises in you is the right way. Remember, meditation, at its core, is daily practice of this sacred pause—and it does take practice.

I've found that learning to quickly read my own fuels and triggers has enabled me to read those of other people, too, so that I can act quickly to create space for them, even before they're aware of the need themselves.

It's All Their Fault

If you are already leading others, watch out for a well-known psychological effect called fundamental attribution error. I hear a lot of leaders complaining about the people on their team, as well as key stakeholders such as marketing, sales, or distribution partners. It seems these folks are always doing things wrong and never, ever listening!

What always follows is the old refrain: *if you want something done right, you have to do it yourself.* I'm here to tell you that your lack of trust is not helping you or your company to grow up big and strong.

The problem stems from the fundamental attribution error, which identifies the tendency to overemphasize personality and underestimate situational explanations when describing someone else's behavior. An example might be when you ask a member of your team to do something and they fail to do it to your satisfaction, you automatically attribute it to a failure of effort, skill, or attitude rather than something else going on with that person or at the company.

That "something going on" may very well be *you.* Ask yourself a few questions first to develop that inward-looking muscle of responsibility to overcome the lack of trust. Here are several examples:

1. Listen to the words you use in association with an employee, such as *should* and *shouldn't* or *can* and *can't.* Using these words, when aimed at someone else, implies that you may be committing the fundamental attribution error.

2. Ask whether you are providing enough clarity around corporate strategy and your expectations for individual team members.

3. Ask whether you're providing clarity for individual team members. At my former company, we designed a delegation tool that made it easy for the *delegate* to ask clarifying questions to the delegator (you) about scope, deadlines, and the like. Assignments that are well structured stand a better chance of being successful.

4. Finally, think hard about building in regular checkpoints that establish a communication rhythm for you and your team. These may include quarterly town halls where you provide big picture updates, monthly meetings where you dive deeper into your key performance indicators (KPIs) and other matters, and even weekly meetings or voice memos to those who report to and/or are working on special projects for you.

The next time you feel your frustration rising over an employee's performance, ask yourself:

- Am I expecting too much of this person?
- Am I expecting them to think like a manager when I hired them as a worker bee?
- Am I expecting them to think strategically and long-term like a VP even though they have zero experience doing that kind of work?

If the answer to any of these questions is yes, perhaps you haven't done your job of putting people in the right roles. Think about reassigning the project or task to somebody else with the right kind of skill and experience. But ultimately take 100% ownership of the problem, which doesn't mean doing it yourself.

What Integrity Actually Means in Practice

There's a state that conscious leadership describes as being "in integrity." When you're in integrity, you're doing what you're supposed to be doing—you are fulfilling your purpose in this world. And when you're fulfilling your purpose, your energy flows naturally and renews itself. What's more, the whole world seems to align with you and conspire for your benefit.

A couple of years ago, I completed the Conscious Leadership Group's 15 Commitments Coaching Certification program, which involved 13 months of intensive work with the Conscious Leadership Group that supports organizational coaches. I did it because I wanted to bring these tools to the founders with whom I worked in my role (at the time) as managing partner at Findaway Adventures.

The whole point of conscious leadership is to live a life, including a professional life, of integrity. When you reach that point, you feel as though you are in the flow, using your superpowers every day, unencumbered by the fight or flight emotional states that can take hold of you when they do the least amount of good.

So, what does it mean to live life in integrity? Integrity includes four pillars: emotional intelligence, impeccable agreements, healthy responsibility, and conscious communication. To be "out of integrity" is to have feelings we don't feel, commitments we don't keep, responsibilities we don't own, and truths we don't say.

When I work with companies on developing their purpose and vision, our work always brings us to the topic of core values. When developing core values, you should not settle for describing things you stand for—rather, you should describe concrete ways of behaving and delivering on your commitments to others. One of the most popular core values is integrity, which its adopters roughly intend to mean "honest, truthful, and well intentioned."

But this meaning misses an important application of the word *integrity*.

The next time someone asks you to do something and you drop every-thing and do it, to the detriment of your or your team's mental health, ask yourself: "Am I out of integrity?" Only then, after you've answered the question honestly and to your satisfaction, should you make your decision to do it or not.

When I see a business owner who expresses frustration, anger, ex-haustion, or overwhelm with regard to their employees, I see somebody who is likely behaving out of integrity. A leader who is out of integrity will infect his or her entire team, creating a *vicious cycle* of finger-pointing and frustration. The truth is fairly simple: if your team isn't honoring their commitments and agreements with themselves and one another, they're probably following your lead.

Acting in integrity means taking responsibility for our feelings and speaking the truth. Those who operate in integrity feel an energetic whole-ness that comes from feeling in sync with their thoughts and emotions. More often than not, their teams will feed off this positive energy, which creates a *virtuous cycle* of honesty and positivity, even when disagreements are on the table.

I've experienced being both in and out of integrity, and let me tell you, being *in* feels a whole lot better than *out*. There is more energy for me and everyone around me. But it takes work, starting with knowing the things that typically block integrity. As the Conscious Leadership Group has taught me, there are four major blockages that cut off this energy, not unlike how a dead bulb on a string of lights disrupts the flow of energy to the other lights. As we noted earlier in this section, these blockages include:

1. Responsibilities we don't own
2. Feelings we don't feel
3. Truths we don't say
4. Agreements we don't keep

I'll bet the next time you find yourself involved in some kind of company drama that saps your energy, you can trace it to one of these blockages rather than to the shortcomings or misbehaviors of someone else.

To return to our example of the leader who is always willing to drop everything, they are out of integrity because they are not prioritizing what's most important for the business. Or they may be dishonoring their own rhythm, need for sleep, need for exercise, or desire for family time.

Leaders can be the world's greatest agreement breakers because they excel at telling themselves stories about how busy they are and how right they are about what is best for their businesses. When something comes up that seems more important than what they said they would do, they do it without a second thought.

Except that the new thing is usually not that important after all, while doing it throws the rest of their team out of whack and, just maybe, undermines the team's trust in the leader. That's being out of integrity.

I also see business owners who often show up late for meetings, which they explain by telling themselves stories about their own importance and ability to react to an emergency when it pops up. It's the "nobody knows the troubles I've seen" complex. So, they are late, setting a tone for the whole company who are likely to begin thinking, *Hey, I'm pretty busy, too, so I'll play fast and loose with schedules and deadlines.*

This behavior drives the business owner crazy. For these companies, I suggest another core value—irony.

But seriously, I challenge business owners to set the tone for staying in integrity, which requires setting clear agreements with themselves and how they are going to behave. Then, they need to set clear agreements with their team by setting up a corporate calendar rhythm for the year. Creating this kind of meeting rhythm enables leaders to set clear expectations for meeting start times and to determine who is doing what and by when—the foundation for successful agreements.

Once the business owner sets the integrity tone for the company, magical things happen. Suddenly, there's plenty of energy to go around. The joy and the creativity that fill the individual leader also fill the company. And suddenly, all those little fires that used to pop up everywhere—emergency after emergency that the business owner chases down—all start to disappear.

Of course, leaders will always face genuine emergencies that require them to renegotiate their agreements with their team. But this should be the exception rather than the rule.

Be a Force Multiplier

Dan Sullivan and Benjamin Hardy's book *10x Is Easier Than 2x: How World-Class Entrepreneurs Achieve More by Doing Less* argues that setting breakthrough "10x" goals forces us to achieve a clarity and focus that makes achieving them easier than achieving smaller, incremental "2x" goals. Smaller goals give us too many options to choose from; breakthrough goals force us to pick a pathway and stick to it. As Sullivan explains:

> This is because going 2x is not enough growth or enough of an incentive to really make a difference in your life. With 2x growth, an increase in income means an increase in time and effort. You'd be working longer and harder, but not smarter. 10x growth, on the other hand, requires working less than you are now. It requires real change in the way you operate. It means a total transformation of how you run your business in order to include more teamwork and more delegation so that you're personally freed up to focus on what you do best: innovating and providing the vision for your company.

This argument makes sense, as do the authors' caveat that while breakthrough goals might be easier in many respects, they are also scarier because focus—commitment to going deep on one thing and achieving *mastery*, to use their word—doesn't come naturally to most people. This brings us back to the need for boldness, or *courage*, to use Sullivan and Hardy's word, which is a necessary component of an abundant mindset and supports the belief that we can all develop to our full potential—and that potential is probably 10x what we think it is.

When you have an abundance mindset, you think in terms of being *willing* to do things rather than merely *wanting* to do them. You take radical responsibility for what happens *by* you rather than *to* you. That means if you're losing sales, it's because you have been 100% committed to losing sales—and vice versa. Going all in on your big purpose rather than picking away at the low-hanging fruit requires you to fight through some fear, but once you do this and take responsibility for your outcomes, you become a force multiplier who will attract other like-minded and brave-souled individuals.

The late, great founder and author Jim Rohn is credited with formulating the idea that "you are the average of the five people you spend the most time with," a phrase that has been widely used by others. If you're hanging out with go-getters, you're likely going to be a go-getter. And if you hang out with wannabes, you'll likely be one of those, instead. It's easier to find your superpowers when you're around people who have already found their superpowers—or who show an interest in discovering them. It's easier to set change-the-world goals when your own passion for those goals acts like a North Star that everyone who comes into your sphere of influence can see, feel, and understand, and from which they can draw inspiration.

Once you adopt an abundance mindset, you cannot help but become a force multiplier. You become contagiously impactful to not only others but also yourself. Witness Jordan Rubin, who founded two companies after Garden of Life. Witness yours truly, who has founded two companies since leaving MegaFood and am now writing the words you are reading on this page. Yes, there is something magical about the power of mindset, but changing your mindset is also something of a science or, at the very least, a methodology. It involves creating your personal flight plan.

Your Personal Flight Plan

Years ago, I found inspiration from reading Patrick Lencioni's *The Advantage*, which presents a framework for fostering organizational clarity around defining your purpose, values, value proposition, priorities, and measures of success. If you're steering a company, you're likely no stranger to the power of strategic planning, right? Blueprints and flight plans are indispensable tools for aligning your organization with its objectives and purpose. The plan is the result of collective hard work, providing you the essential space to navigate your business endeavors (we explore this more in stage 2).

I asked myself whether I might extend that same dedication to crafting a personal flight plan or life plan. It seemed an intriguing notion. After all, a purpose-driven leader follows one path that covers both professional and personal domains. I formulated a personal flight plan to act as a compass I keep within arm's reach that adapts organizational principles for personal contexts. The following questions are a starting point for formulating a Personal Flight Plan:

1. **What's pivotal in my life?** The theme for me now is "a new chapter" in personal and professional life as we make ScalePassion viable and sustainable, and as my wife, Dianna, and I get used to being empty nesters. Renewed focus on my short-term and long-term health.

2. **Why do I exist?** We did this work in chapter 2. Mine is: I exist to improve the world by helping others (e.g., change-the-world

leaders, my wife, friends, other CEOs, all leaders) scale their impact—personally and through their companies.

3. **What do I *do*?** This mirrors the essence of a mission statement, encompassing service, quality, and intangible contributions. Mine describes my key commitments to delivering results this way: To deliver results, I am present. I listen. I provide vision. I inspire. I align. I coach. I lead. I am relentless in my pursuit of learning and adding value to the lives and enterprises of others.

4. **How do I behave?** This mirrors corporate values but extends to your personal brand. It encapsulates how you treat others and how you aim to be perceived. For me: I strive to live a life of high integrity by being conscious, present, enlightened, and committed to driving results. I have the courage to say what needs to be said from a place of love by speaking my truth clearly and understandably. I want to inspire people with my joy and win their trust through keeping my agreements.

5. **What is my zone of genius?** This is what you are best at and never tire of doing. For me: scaling impact—my own, others, team, organizations. I do this through teaching, mentoring, speaking publicly, learning, team building, strategic planning, problem-solving, envisioning the future, and mapping how to attain it.

6. **What are my triggers and fuel?** Triggers incite your fight or flight response, while fuel ignites positivity, bringing forth your optimal self. For me: My fuel includes connecting in a deep way with people through teaching, mentoring, strategic planning, and the other activities in my zone of genius. Also spending quality time with my wife. My triggers include slow cars in the left lane, people who don't listen or try to connect and understand me, and feeling isolated.

7. **Where is this heading?** Attach tangible figures to your aspirations and visions. Set financial milestones for your family and

professional objectives for your business. Picture a thriving life for you and your loved ones in 5, 10, or 20 years. For me, I want to be considered the best in the world at driving the social impact of leaders and companies through my company, writing, international speaking, and media influence and leading a top 10% podcast.

8. **What is most important right now?** Priorities evolve and should include commitments to personal and professional growth. My priorities include keeping my energy and focus, staying in my zone of genius, exercising regularly, spending time with Dianna, working to meet deadlines for my first book, and successfully navigating ScalePassion through its first phase.

9. **What are my immediate next steps?** Every plan requires a list of concrete steps to realize the desired outcomes. Compile a range of options and assign the necessary actions. Execute and validate your progress. Examples of this for me at the time of this writing might include: build a community of five thousand to support the book launch; get my second edits to the editor, Katie, by June 20; and follow an 18:6 fast for five days out of the week.

Put aside an hour or two and draft your own personal flight plan for your life, including how you might use your business to support your personal ambition to improve the world. The worst that can happen is you'll see life more completely than you did before. And the best thing that can happen is that, much like Ethan Holmes, you'll discover that creating greater impact through your business also creates greater business growth and success.

Lew's Tips & Resources

I think Dad's three maxims all lead to mindset. Some could argue that mindset could be the first of the superpowers, but I think he would have wanted it as the capstone. Purpose drives energy, energy facilitates focus, and the great catalyst that keeps it all spiraling up is mindset.

Maxim 1: Make a Difference

- **Your mindset sets the tone:** As a leader, your attitude and outlook directly impact your company's culture and success.
- **Embrace an abundance mindset:** Believe in a world of plenty where growth and success are attainable for all.
- **Take responsibility:** Recognize that your mindset shapes your reality and commit to owning your outcomes.

Maxim 2: Be Bold

- **Confront fear:** Boldly face the fears that hold you back from embracing an abundance mindset and taking responsibility for your actions.
- **Practice conscious leadership:** Cultivate the courage to pause, reflect, and respond thoughtfully to triggers and challenges.
- **Set breakthrough goals:** Dare to aim for 10x growth instead of settling for incremental progress, and commit to pursuing your big purpose with unwavering boldness.

Maxim 3: Do It Right

- **Foster self-awareness:** Regularly assess your triggers and fuels to gain insights into your emotional habits and reactions.

- **Avoid the fundamental attribution error:** Instead of blaming others for shortcomings, examine your own role and leadership in shaping outcomes.
- **Surround yourself with growth-minded individuals:** Seek out a network of like-minded individuals who inspire and challenge you to reach your full potential.
- **Craft your personal flight plan:** Don't wait; get started on this.

Books or Articles to Consider

- *15 Commitments of Conscious Leadership* by Jim Dethmer, Diana Chapman, and Kaley Klemp
- *10x Is Easier Than 2x* by Dan Sullivan and Benjamin Hardy
- *The Advantage* by Patrick Lencioni

Tools to Consider

- Headspace meditation app (headspace.com)
- Waking Up meditation app (wakingup.com)

Scale Passion Resources

- *Your Personal Flight Plan* workbook: a do-it-yourself guide for harnessing your personal purpose
- "The Green Sheet Delegation Approach": a guide for teaching delegation across your organization

Find a comprehensive list of resources at ScalePassion.com/Resources.

Keys to Stage 1

Don't Gloss Over Personal Leadership

Okay, just a quick reset here. I want to emphasize that you must first be able to harness your personal purpose and lead yourself before you can lead others and scale that purpose. It is so important for you to have a firm grasp on your own purpose—your reason for being on this planet—before you attempt to inject that purpose into the company or team you are leading.

I am aware you are likely to move past this stage and into stage 2 of this book without first doing the work on your purpose, energy, focus, and mindset, just like I might while reading on a plane, but at the very least, take one or two of the following next steps before turning the page:

- Buy one of the recommended books and dig in—get inspired.
- Download a meditation app and schedule 15 minutes per day to start practicing at the ideal time for you.
- Visit www.scalepassion.com/resources and download one of the recommended worksheets or take a personal leadership assessment at www.changetheworldleader.com to help you map your journey.

- Start by simply writing your draft purpose statement here: "I exist to _____."

Do you feel that energy? See how this simple statement can help focus everything going forward? Can you understand the mindset shift you will need to make to see this purpose through?

Take some action right now before diving into stage 2, "Scale the Business Purpose and Lead Others with Integrity."

SCALE THE BUSINESS PURPOSE AND LEAD OTHERS WITH INTEGRITY

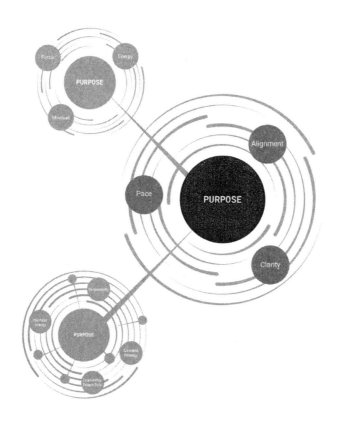

Chapter 6

The Foundation for Scale

D o you remember meeting Jeff Byers, the former NFL lineman and cofounder of Momentous in chapter 3? When I began working with him and his cofounder, Erica, they would have described themselves as completely aligned. And, to a large extent, they were. The problem they were experiencing was that no one else on their team was aligned in quite the same way as they were. Jeff and Erica were operating on a totally different level of understanding and passion than their employees.

When I met them, they thought their team "just wasn't getting it," but it didn't take long before these two leaders realized they were the ones who weren't getting it. "Founders typically move at a very different level," admitted Jeff. "We were so busy doing what we were doing that we never considered we weren't communicating with our team in a way they could understand and react to. We understood what we meant, so we figured they would too."

While the company was making money, its culture was far from sustainable, which meant the company was far from stable. When I began working with them, the first thing I did was sit down with them and ask them to slow down, take a breath or 10, and tell me about themselves and their project. And while it was clear to me that Jeff and Erica were in sync, it grew equally clear that the company lacked a broader synchronicity—the kind that can only happen once the business owner has taken the time and effort to scale their senior leadership alongside their purpose and passion.

And so we worked on taking that passion and leadership style and pulling it out so that it could lead others as well as the cofounders. Too few companies do this. They just assume that their teams will eventually get it, absorbing the values, culture, and purpose of the business owners. But that's not the way it works. At Momentous, we discovered that Erica and Jeff's core values—such as grit and inclusivity—weren't serving them in any meaningful way because the words alone didn't describe actual, expected behaviors.

"They were basically table stakes," observed Jeff.

So, we developed values that connected the dots between values and behaviors, such as "bias toward action, drive to win, and lead consciously and make an impact." We also went deep into understanding Momentous's ideal customer, whom we gave the name Sam, suitably androgynous.

"We had never given our customer a name because we had never really explored Sam together as a team," recalled Jeff. "When your team doesn't have a shared understanding of your customer, decisions don't make sense. How could they?"

"Sam is not an athlete," noted Jeff. "Sam cares about longevity, health, and wellness as a whole, which includes exercise, sleep, work life, diet, and various lifestyle choices. They make conscious decisions every day, so we want them to have access to the best science-based thinking out there. Some of them are weekend warriors; many are not. We wanted them to benefit from the kind of information only elite athletes get. Their goals may be to be happy and healthier rather than compete in the Olympics, but they deserve the best too."

We came up with a big, hairy, audacious goal (BHAG), which was to fundamentally change the dietary supplement category of high performance, which Jeff and Erica believed had been broken because of lack of trust, transparency, and regulation. "Too many loopholes and too much snake oil," was how Jeff phrased it. So, the founders went out and recruited scientists to help them clean up the category, and before they knew it, they were not only selling their supplements direct to consumers and pro and college sports teams and organizations but also working with private and public organizations to fund federal research on nutrition and supplements.

We also helped Jeff and Erica take their deep understanding of their purpose—to democratize high performance in life and fitness—and make it accessible to every member of their team in a personal and actionable way. For example, Momentous attracted (and continues to attract) highly skilled and qualified employees who happened to be elite athletes, including an Olympic-caliber marathoner who could see exactly how his role as vice president of products contributed to democratizing high performance. Eventually, every team member could begin to see how they fit in with this purpose and what contribution they could make. And you know what? Some didn't see the fit and parted ways with Momentous. But that was good for them and Momentous because we had removed the drama and helped everyone see what really mattered and was most important to the culture.

Taking the time to create clarity in this way may have momentarily slowed things down for the company, but it rewired it to go faster once the strategy was in place. The company is still rowing up a fast-moving river, but instead of doing it in six different boats, it's doing it in a single boat and everyone is rowing together. Jeff says that while Momentous could probably have "fought and punched" its way to where it is today, it would have been far more stressful and taken a much larger toll on his team.

"What we have now is a more sustainable pathway to growth," Jeff said. "And by sustainable, I mean now that we've done the work of laying out our strategy, values, customer, why, and priorities, we can use this to hire people who align with our purpose, instead of just plugging holes."

Plugging holes. Too many business owners have hired me to help them plug holes when what they really needed to do was build a team. That's what this section of the book is about, building out your leadership team like Momentous has done: through purpose, clarity, alignment, and pace.

Giant Shoulders

In stage 1, we focused on harnessing the purpose of the business owner as the prerequisite for leading others in the construction of a truly purpose-driven company. If you are reading this book, I am going to make certain assumptions about you. For example, I assume you believe it would be incredibly fulfilling to build a company, team, or start-up that could do good in the world, grow, and make money. I'm even going to assume that, before you read this book, you had already heard of ideas like conscious capitalism and creating shared value.

This book isn't about convincing you to build or rebuild a high-impact business; it's about suggesting ways you might do it once you feel the call to make a difference, be bold, and do it right. That said, I do want to position my how-to approach within a broader framework because, in writing this book, I have stood on the shoulders of giants just as surely as Isaac Newton claimed to have done in his famous 1675 letter to Robert Hooke.

People tell me I'm the consummate early adopter when it comes to technology and innovative ideas. I suppose I'm guilty as charged, but I've always hungered for growth and have pursued new ways of thinking every chance I get. When I refer to the term *conscious capitalism*, it's because I was one of the people in the audience when John Mackey, the cofounder and CEO of Whole Foods Market, talked about conscious capitalism at the 2014 Conscious Capitalism CEO Summit in Austin, Texas.

The difference between me and some other folks is that I went back home and tried to put his ideas to work! Like many people, I choose not to follow any one school of thought or to be doctrinaire when it comes to applying theory to practice. I mix and match to fit the organizational structure and resources of the company I'm leading or coaching.

In Austin, I spent three days eating barbecue and talking and listening to the top leaders in the conscious capitalism movement. Both John Mackey and Raj Sisodia, who founded Conscious Capitalism Inc., spoke about this new idea of enlarging the number of stakeholders beyond Milton Friedman's narrow focus on maximizing profits for shareholders. They spoke (and wrote in *Conscious Capitalism: Liberating the Heroic Spirit of Business*) that business should have a higher purpose than simply making money. And they put their faith in corporate culture as the medium for accomplishing this more holistic approach to business. They advocated for business owners developing soft skills, such as empathy, emotional intelligence, and integrity, as the basis for creating cultures based on trust, collaboration, and empowerment rather than pure transactional value.

It was during this same period that I attended Michael Porter's seminar on creating shared value (CSV) and first heard about the concept of social enterprise, the intersection of societal needs, corporate assets and expertise, and business opportunity. Both CSV and conscious capitalism represented, at least to my eyes, far deeper and bolder alternatives for change than did corporate social responsibility (CSR), which I've taken to mean acknowledging responsibility for things like recycling, power efficiency, corporate governance issues, and environmentalism writ large.

CSR is far easier to fake than CSV or conscious capitalism because its integration into strategy isn't required. This is why so many firms open themselves, quite rightly it has turned out, to accusations of greenwashing or virtue signaling. What I'm suggesting in this book is that we go a step further or deeper than CSV or conscious capitalism to pull the organization's purpose out of the ethos of the founder, entrepreneur, or leader and bake it into the brand or company. This is what differentiates the Scale Passion Method from CSV, CSR, and other types of social-impact concepts. It's not a template or overlay to your company; it's an organic process of unleashing purpose and then building a company that can scale that purpose.

I had always been more or less unconsciously oriented toward purpose-driven leadership and companies. That was certainly the case at Garden of Life, where I was so inspired by Jordan's mission to help people improve their health. When I went to MegaFood and became involved in conscious leadership, I began to put words and concepts around my natural inclinations. At the Conscious Capitalism CEO Summit, I found myself sitting next to Brian Robertson, author of *Holacracy: The Revolutionary Management System That Abolishes Hierarchy*, and several CEOs who were practicing it. According to *Holacracy*, companies can operate more nimbly and responsively when decision-making power is distributed around the organization. A full Holacracy replaces job titles, hierarchies, and rigid departmental structures with a constitution that runs the company, which is organized as a structure of circles. Each circle has four requirements: purpose, strategy, domain, and accountability. Everyone in the company belongs to one or more circles. Staff contributions are defined by their roles within a circle. Free of fixed (and often outdated or irrelevant) job titles, circle members can have discrete roles within different circles.

When I returned to MegaFood, we implemented a hybrid version of Holacracy we called Holacracy Lite, based on the work of Robertson and the work of economist and Harvard Business School professor Rosabeth Moss Kanter, which advocated for a blend of hierarchical management and cross-functional teaming. Although MegaFood wasn't culturally or strategically positioned to adopt Holacracy wholesale, implementing a tailored version allowed us to accomplish our pivot from a retail focus to consumer focus much faster than we would otherwise have done.

At a CSV symposium at Harvard, where I sat beside representatives from organizations like Toyota and the Bill & Melinda Gates Foundation,

I was riveted by white papers and case studies; by the second day, I was mapping out what we'd do at MegaFood. One of the first things I did back home was hiring the company's first vice president of social impact, Sara Newmark, and putting a team behind her. With Sara leading the charge, we obtained B Corp certification, which introduced new practices in every corner of the company, provided amazing guardrails for our social-impact-focused growth, and transformed the brand.

As I said, I'm an early and enthusiastic adopter, but the takeaway here is that the best thing you can do is learn from those who went deep into these philosophies, tried them, made some mistakes along the way, and learned from them, then try them out on your terms. Be flexible in your thinking, and regard these ideas as tools you can use to make a difference. Don't view them as a religion or gospel. Don't be a strict constructionist but adapt the ideas to your life and business. And don't be afraid to try things and fail—this is where all the learning is.

There is a significant transition happening—from an output economy to an impact economy—and I believe it is going to unleash many different purposes: from a passion to reduce plastic in our seas to supporting farmers or small-town America to ending domestic violence or improving the health of expectant mothers in developing countries. And if you don't believe in climate change, and I do, and you are focused on teaching entrepreneurism to inner-city youth, and I'm not, we can still be part of the same movement to broaden the number of stakeholders who benefit from our businesses.

And if you're an entrepreneur who has only five people on your team and you can pay them better than what they can make someplace else, you're making a difference in those people's lives. Welcome aboard. The critical point is, no matter what type of difference we are focused on, as business owners, we can (and I would say we are obligated to) make that difference.

Beyond "Git 'er Done!"

Capitalism's evolution includes businesses with different passions and purposes, and so should these businesses include different kinds of people on their teams. Most change-the-world entrepreneurs I know have specific, high expectations for the people around them. The problem is that people don't often meet these expectations. This can be very frustrating for a business owner and put a serious crimp in a company's morale, not to mention prospects for success.

Years ago, I consulted with an entrepreneur who was feeling frustrated in this way, and we ended up exploring the different types of people in terms of their general strengths in the workplace. I came up with four types of people: doers, thinkers, planners, and creatives.

The entrepreneur I was speaking with immediately saw a pattern: her company was full of doers but lacked thinkers, planners, and creatives—to her company's detriment. Entrepreneurs of early-stage companies tend to attract doers who are personally connected to the entrepreneur's powerful, specific vision. The doers align with that vision and pour their energies into helping the entrepreneur realize the vision.

These doers might even be friends, family, or cause-oriented people who will jump in the foxhole and get stuff done. They're critical to growing a company and valuable to have around. The problem comes when the entrepreneur gets overwhelmed with being the sole or chief decision-maker for everything, or when the company gets big enough that the entrepreneur needs people who can help think and plan.

To be successful and scale the business, an entrepreneur also needs to have a thinker on the team, somebody who really likes to think things through as far as where the company can or ought to go. A thinker will have well-reasoned and innovative ideas about new product development or new channels to explore or new buyer personas that were overlooked in the early days of the start-up. The vice president of research and development at my former company was a thinker whom I depended on for his instincts and experience with regard to a period when the company was rapidly growing and introducing new products.

At first blush, you might think that thinking and planning are the same thing. They can be, but being one or the other does not guarantee that you'll be the other. The planner is more concerned with the "how" and "when" than the "what" and "why," which are the thinker's focus. Planners are comfortable planning six months or even a year or more in the future. They take in the vision and then lay out a strategy and budget for seeing it through to completion.

Last but not least, the creative leaps to the fore whenever talk turns to telling the brand's story in words, visuals, or both. Your creative people are good at taking abstract ideas and turning them into compelling and consistent stories that span every area of the company. At MegaFood, for example, our creative people turned all our core values and "farm to tablet" narrative into a unified message that resonated in our marketing, design, website development, packaging, culture, and so on.

The important thing to remember here is that few individuals possess all four of these personality types. Yes, some doers can also plan, and some thinkers may have a creative streak. But the entrepreneur shouldn't count on running his or her company by relying on a few jack-of-all-trades. Entrepreneurs need to do their assessment work in light of these special talents and gifts before trying to assign tasks to people who aren't wired to achieve them to the leader's standards.

Remember, it's not enough to have people who can "cover" marketing, sales, operations, finance, and so on. You also want to achieve a diversity of approaches to problem-solving and decision-making that cut across the disciplines. It's all a part of scaling a change-the-world business.

From Autocracy to Accountability

How's that for an eye-grabbing subhead? Let's unpack it. The cultures of most companies and many of the teams I've worked with that have successfully scaled their impact evolve through four stages: autocracy, accountability, autonomy, and responsibility. Once you've done the work of learning to unleash your personal purpose, energy, and focus, your job as the business owner is to lead your team through each of these phases. In this section of the book, we'll focus on the first two phases, autocracy and accountability, before turning to autonomy and responsibility in stage 3.

In autocracy, the business owner is making practically all the decisions and certainly *all* the important decisions. In autocracy, the energy and focus emanate from the leader like a thousand suns. Founders never tire of talking about their babies at work, at home, and to anyone who will listen. The business owner is the articulator in chief of the company's purpose, mission, and values. The leader's faith and sheer force of willpower will get the business through the start-up and early growth phases but will eventually burn itself out if the business owner hasn't made the effort to scale these titanic forces within the organization by replacing autocracy with accountability.

In an accountable culture, the business owner is actively enlisting the engagement of others to create clarity around the company's purpose, values, mission, and vision so that others can become accountable for following them. An accountable culture is built around a leadership team rather than a single leader, which means the leader has to learn to give up some decision-making power in exchange for the injection of diverse talent and brainpower. An accountable culture focuses on driving clear expectations and metrics to set and evaluate goals and progress.

A big part of transitioning from autocracy to accountability involves hiring the right kinds of people for your culture and, once they're on board, keeping them rowing in the same direction. And it all begins with, you guessed it, clearly articulating your purpose. This is closely followed by the clarity that comes from generating a great strategy, alignment around that strategy, and a pace that honors the long-term nature of pursuing the purpose.

Let's get to it.

Lew's Tips & Resources

No one worked harder than Lew Craven. He was also wise. As we outline how to build a change-the-world company that connects deeply with your personal purpose, channel your inner Lew and do the hard work of building your company on a foundation of purpose, clarity, alignment, and pace. There are no shortcuts. No prefab kits. As Lew would say, "You've got to do it right."

Maxim 1: Make a Difference

- **Adopt purpose-driven leadership:** By focusing on unleashing purpose, leaders can ensure that their businesses are making a positive impact on the world.
- **Learn from management philosophies:** Learning from management philosophies like conscious capitalism and creating shared value can provide business owners with frameworks for creating companies that prioritize making a difference in addition to profits.

Maxim 2: Be Bold

- **Balance team composition:** Business owners need to be bold in assembling teams with diverse skill sets and personalities to tackle challenges from different angles.
- **Evolve your organizational culture:** Transitioning from autocracy to accountability requires bold leadership to empower team members and distribute decision-making authority.

Maxim 3: Do It Right

- **Generate clarity around purpose, values, and mission:** Ensuring clarity around the company's purpose, values, and mission helps leaders do things right by aligning their actions with their core principles.

- **Adopt appropriate management philosophies:** Business owners must adapt management philosophies to fit their company's context and ensure that they are implemented correctly to drive positive change.

Books or Articles to Consider
- "Creating Shared Value" by Michael Porter and Mark Kramer
- *Conscious Capitalism* by John Mackey and Raj Sisodia
- *Abundance* by Peter Diamandis and Steven Kotler
- *10x Is Easier Than 2x* by Dan Sullivan and Benjamin Hardy

Scale Passion Resources
- "Are You Ready to Scale?" assessment: a simple online survey that will help you map your gaps to scaling purpose
- "A Scorecard for the Change-the-World Leader": map your personal leadership journey of scaling purpose

Find a comprehensive list of resources at ScalePassion.com/Resources.

Chapter 7

Key #1: Choose Purpose over Mission

n January of 2003, I participated in a 40-day group exercise called Purpose Driven Life that was offered through my church, which I was active in at the time. About 24 days into the program, I experienced nothing short of an epiphany, which told me in crystal-clear terms that my purpose in life was to become a change-the-world CEO. Since that time, I have devoted myself to scaling passion both in my own businesses and in those where I served as CEO. My passion to help others scale their passion helped me choose which companies to start or join as well as how to lead them.

When I joined MegaFood, for example, I wasn't particularly passionate about supplements or farmers, but I *was* passionate about scaling a business that looked as though it could do good in the world. Once I settled into the leadership role there, I began to see how the ingredients that went into the supplements were raised by small farmers who had their own challenges competing against industrial agriculture. As MegaFood grew in revenue and employees, I attracted (and pursued) people who aligned with the idea of supporting small, family-owned, often organic farming businesses, which, in turn, attracted some remarkable people. One was a woman named Sara Newmark, whom you met in chapter 6. Sara helped move MegaFood into a national leadership position on soil health for our industry, especially in the company's public stance against the use of glyphosate in farming practices.

But the input that really got me moving in the direction of activism came not from the farmers but our customers who were telling us, thanks to the market research we did, that they wanted us to lend our voice to reforming conventional farming practices. My purpose of scaling impact motivated me to take the feedback from customers and use my platform as CEO to push for moving the company in that direction. If I wasn't passionate about scaling impact, I may have found reasons to ignore our customers.

If you're a start-up entrepreneur, a vice president, a team leader, the leader and CEO of a thriving mature business, or the CEO of a multibillion-dollar company, ask yourself how you can tie your own personal story and purpose into the purpose of the company. As we discussed in chapter 3, the energy this will give you will enable you to attract others to your cause. This was the point of stage 1: once you align with your personal purpose, you can bring the energy and focus it gives you to practically any organization you choose to join, transforming it.

Stage 2 provides the tools and concepts you can use to successfully scale your purpose with your leadership team, which, as we'll see in stage 3, cascades to all levels of the organization.

At MegaFood, all we did to put ourselves on this pathway was to agree—and here I must offer a debt of gratitude to Patrick Lencioni—that our reason for existing wasn't simply to be the best darn manufacturer of "quality" supplements but rather to aspire to change the world. The key word here, as Lencioni has argued, is *aspire*.

Embrace the Aspiration

"All you need to know is that your company exists to do something magical in this world. Something inspired. Your company needs to serve to make the world a better place," Patrick Lencioni writes in *The Advantage*. "Anything less is not acceptable, boring and unsustainable."

One of the world's greatest purpose-driven companies is Patagonia, which manufacturers outdoor apparel, equipment, and more recently, a selection of camping cuisine. On September 14, 2022, the iconic business announced new ownership nearly 50 years after founder Yvon Chouinard started the company. "Effective immediately," the company press release said, "the Chouinard family has transferred all ownership to two new entities: Patagonia Purpose Trust and the Holdfast Collective. Most significantly, every dollar that is not reinvested back into Patagonia will be distributed as dividends to protect the planet."

In other words, observed Chouinard, who is now the company's board chair, from that point on, "Instead of extracting value from nature and transforming it into wealth, we are using the wealth Patagonia creates to protect the source. *We're making Earth our only shareholder.* I am dead serious about saving this planet."

Feel that passion? Feel that energy?

The company projects that it will pay out an annual dividend of roughly $100 million, depending on the health of the business. Now, that's what you call putting your purse strings behind your purpose!

But the larger point I want to make is that Patagonia didn't start out as a world changer—not by a long shot. Chouinard started out as a technical expert in climbing, hunting, fishing, falconry, and other outdoor pursuits. He and his hiking buddies used to hide from park rangers in Yosemite so they could enjoy the park longer. After purchasing a coal forge, he sold homemade pitons and carabiners out of his car up and down the California coast. He was a designer at heart, so he originally named his company Chouinard Equipment.

Originally, achieving "perfection" in design was the principal goal. But as the company grew, this focus began to not so much change—the company that would become Patagonia still prided itself in building durable products—but rather take on an additional purpose. The company began making their clothes lighter on the body and easier on the landscape, replacing the destructive pilons, for example, with less damaging anchors. Over the years, Chouinard took his leadership teams back to the Argentine region of Patagonia to see how the people and places of that region could inspire the brand. Then he helped foster an organizational culture that inspired his employees to adapt a lifestyle of living and working close to the land at home and at work, encouraging employees to go surfing or climbing during lunch breaks, going barefoot in the office, and offering an on-site day care center to help working families.

As the company thrived, its philanthropic activities were directed at local efforts to preserve a habitat that was used by local peoples: a special stretch of river that was home to steelhead trout, eels, water snakes, and muskrats. Rather than give money to large NGOs with sizable overhead, Patagonia began donating to smaller groups working to save or restore habitats. The company donated 10% of profits each year to these groups, eventually starting the 1% for the Planet initiative in 2002 that enabled other organizations to donate to environmental causes and train their staff on environmental advocacy.

That's a roughly 60-year journey of developing and refining purpose. It didn't happen overnight; it was a natural, organic part of doing good business that grew from a focus on product to a focus on purpose.

In chapter 1, I referenced *Built to Last: Successful Habits of Visionary Companies*, the book where Jim Collins introduced the big, hairy, audacious goal (BHAG) into the business strategy lexicon. I had Collins's book in mind when I sat down to work with a company that provided home fire alarm systems. The company was successful, but the owners felt increasingly adrift as their company grew; they asked me to help them re-center their business around a compelling purpose.

They already had a typical mission—provide reliable fire alarm services to customers—but in the process of learning more about the company, I discovered that the owners were very philanthropic. They focused their philanthropy on causes having to do with displaced children. The more we looked at this seemingly unrelated philanthropic activity, the clearer it became that the company's why—its *purpose*—was to keep people safe. End of story. Or, should I say, beginning of a new story.

"We exist to keep you safe" tells me so much more than an avowal of product quality or even superior service. Again, product and service quality should be a given and constitute a minimum standard for doing business with you. Great companies understand the power of an inspiring purpose to drive growth and value. Ask yourself right now: *If we could do anything as a company that lay at the intersection of our company assets and expertise, a business opportunity, and a social need, what would that look like?* It doesn't have to be about saving the planet. It can simply be about keeping people safe.

Closer to home—very close to home, in fact—my company, Scale-Passion, exists to radically evolve capitalism. Our mission is to support founders and their teams as they scale their purpose-driven businesses. Knowing this has focused us on several priorities or objectives and key results (OKRs), which we'll explore in the next chapter. Right now, our priorities are to build a community of 10 thousand change-the-world leaders and to prepare for a successful book launch—which, if you're reading this book, was successful—to reach even more change-the-world leaders.

Mission and Vision

People often confuse mission and vision for purpose, or vice versa. We shouldn't use the terms interchangeably because doing so will determine how we do—or don't—build purpose and impact into our strategy. So, let's clarify the important differences among these terms before going deep on which ones matter the most.

Mission statements have gotten a bad rap and often deservedly so. Too many of these statements wind up sounding almost identical, allowing for slight differences among industries. Many simply summarize the company's service or product. One of my favorite examples of the latter comes from *The Office*'s fictional paper company, Dunder Mifflin:

> Dunder Mifflin Incorporated provides its customers quality office and information technology products, furniture, printing values, and the expertise required for making informed buying decisions. We provide our products and services with a dedication to the highest degree of integrity and quality of customer satisfaction, developing long-term professional relationships with employees that develop pride, creating a stable working environment and company spirit.

This statement represents the absolute minimum a reputable company should stand for without being closed down. On the other end of the spectrum are companies that try to yoke an arcane technical solution to a larger cause that has nothing to do with what the company does. The sitcom *Silicon Valley* offers hilarious examples of this in its TechCrunch Disrupt spoof in which one leader claims, "We're making the world a better place through software-defined data centers for cloud computing," only to be trumped by another leader's avowed mission "to make the world a better place through scalable, fault-tolerant, distributable databases with ACID transactions."

Here's an easy way to differentiate mission, vision, and purpose:

1. **Mission:** A mission statement describes what your business does, for whom you do it, and how. Your mission focuses on current objectives and approaches to achieving the vision and fulfilling the purpose. By their very nature, missions are action-oriented guides to daily activities. For example, if you are a jet fighter pilot aboard a US aircraft carrier, you may have a *mission* to destroy military installations housing munitions that have been used in attacks against US or ally ships. But your *purpose* is to defend US and allied lives and the United States. That purpose gets handed down through the culture of the military, but it must resonate at some level with each and every member of the armed services in order to work.

    At MegaFood, our mission was: *We keep our customers healthy by providing the world's best supplements made from whole-food ingredients.*

2. **Vision:** A vision statement looks into the future to describe the kind of world you hope to help create and how you see yourself contributing to it. At MegaFood, our vision was: *We envision a world without nutritional poverty—a planet where everyone is truly nourished—we work hard and take bold action to ensure that vision becomes a reality in our lifetime.*

3. **Purpose:** A purpose describes why your business exists besides making a profit—the broader impact you wish to have on customers, employees, your community, and the world. Unlike the mission, the purpose is less action oriented and more inspirational. It aligns with and reinforces your core values and drives long-term direction and goal setting. I'd be happy to hang my hat on any of the following purpose statements from well-known brands (and I did hang my hat on the first!):

    a. "We exist to nourish a world in nutritional crisis." (MegaFood)

    b. "To transform the world into a healthy, sustainable & equitable place for the next seven generations." (Seventh Generation)

c. "To operate the company in a way that actively recognizes the central role that business plays in society by initiating innovative ways to improve the quality of life locally, nationally, and internationally." (Ben & Jerry's)

d. "To inspire and impact the world with vision, purpose, and style. We're constantly asking ourselves how we can do more and make a greater impact—and that starts by reimagining everything that a company and industry can be." (Warby Parker)

e. "We're in business to save our home planet." (Patagonia)

Although a purpose is less action oriented than a mission, it paradoxically carries greater urgency because it takes on bigger challenges with greater implications and outcomes. But here's the instructive point you need to understand: in the case of MegaFood, nourishing a world in nutritional crisis wasn't *my* purpose. It didn't need to come from me to become the company's purpose, but it wouldn't have come to life if I wasn't living my purpose.

Purpose as Energy

The experience of defining your purpose and prioritizing BHAGs around it offers a world-class momentum booster, which was something I discovered at MegaFood. Do you remember the story from the introduction about the major impacts we made at MegaFood? Paying a living wage, partnering with independent farmers, certifying MegaFood as B Corp, practicing conscious leadership company-wide, among other initiatives? That's a picture of what can happen to your company when you double down on your purpose. Over the same period of several years at Mega-Food, we succeeded in leading a national effort to obtain more than 30,000 signatures needed to set in motion legislation to get the weed killer glyphosate banned as a desiccant on oats. That effort included Patagonia and Ben & Jerry's, but it was largely little old MegaFood who led the charge.

Did all this petitioning and social-impact work take our eyes off the economic ball? Not in the least. During this same period, we took the company from $11 million to around $50 million before ultimately selling the business for the highest valuation in the industry at the time. Everybody wanted to be a part of that project. I had senior leaders leave companies where they were making twice as much to become a part of our company. And while we did put in place bonus structures to help them prosper along with the company, those bonuses were literally bonuses—not the only or even main reason we were able to attract them to our team.

Again, the line against some corporate social responsibility claims is that there is little direct relationship between product and passion or purpose. Yet there is no inherent reason that this should be the case. There's a very cool coffee and tea seller named BLK & Bold, a Black-owned brand that donates 5% of its profits to supporting youth nationwide. If you visit the company's website, you find the purpose right there below the company name: "Specialty coffee for you. Impact for our youth."

At BLK & Bold, you cannot buy coffee or tea and *not* support the company's mission: it's baked into the price of the product; it's not an add-on but the product itself. As BLK & Bold says in its e-commerce language, "Shop your values."

It's hard to get any bolder about your purpose!

Digging In on Purpose

Crafting a compelling corporate purpose statement is not just about putting words on a page; it's about defining the soul of your organization.

That's why you have to put your whole soul into scaling it with your team.

Your purpose serves as a guiding light, a shining beacon illuminating the path forward and inspiring both your team and your stakeholders. Here are some key questions to consider as you embark on this journey of purpose discovery:

1. What is your personal purpose? As a founder or entrepreneur, your personal calling can serve as a powerful foundation for your company's purpose. Reflect on what truly drives you, what ignites your passion, and how you can channel that energy into something meaningful through your business.

2. Where do opportunities, assets, and social needs intersect? As creating shared value outlines, consider where your business opportunity intersects with your company's assets and expertise, as well as with the broader social needs of the community or society at large. This intersection is where your purpose lies—a sweet spot where you can create shared value and make a tangible difference in the world.

3. What is your broader impact? Think beyond your immediate business goals and explore the broader impact your work could have on society, the environment, and the community. How can your company contribute positively to these larger issues? How can you leverage your resources and influence to drive meaningful change?

4. How does your work connect to societal and environmental issues? Examine the role your company plays in addressing these challenges. How can you align your purpose with efforts to create a more sustainable and equitable world?

Delve deep into these questions and engage in thoughtful introspection to uncover the true essence of your company's purpose. Embrace this process as an opportunity to align your business with your values, passions, and aspirations. Remember, your purpose is not just a statement—it's a guiding principle that can shape the trajectory of your organization and leave a lasting impact on the world.

Lew's Tips & Resources

When I was five, my big career plan was to be a garbageman because they got to wear gloves and hang off the back of the truck all day. My dad would say, "Son, I don't care what you do when you grow up, but I want you to always make a difference." The connection between your personal purpose and the company's is the spark that lights the fuse of impact.

Maxim 1: Make a Difference

- **Choose purpose over mission:** Distinguish between mission, vision, and purpose. Mission statements often lack inspiration and fail to articulate a deeper *why*. Purpose goes beyond current objectives and approaches, describing the broader impact a company wishes to have on customers, employees, the community, and the world.
- **Channel personal purpose:** Reflect on your personal purpose as a founder or entrepreneur. Your personal calling can serve as a powerful foundation for your company's purpose.
- **Locate the intersection of opportunity, assets, and social need:** Identify where your business opportunity intersects with your company's assets and expertise, as well as broader social needs. This intersection is where your purpose lies—a sweet spot for creating shared value and making a tangible difference.

Maxim 2: Be Bold

- **Seek broader impact:** Consider the broader impact your work could have on society, the environment, and the community.

Explore how your company can contribute positively to these larger issues and drive meaningful change.

- **Inspire purpose:** Craft a compelling corporate purpose statement that defines the soul of your organization. Put your whole soul into scaling it with your team.
- **Take bold actions:** Take bold actions aligned with your purpose. Don't be afraid to challenge the status quo and pursue initiatives that reflect your company's values and aspirations.
- **Align with values:** Embrace the process of aligning your business with your values, passions, and aspirations. Your purpose is not just a statement—it's a guiding principle that can shape the trajectory of your organization.

Maxim 3: Do It Right

- **Differentiate clearly:** Clearly differentiate between mission, vision, and purpose to avoid confusion and ensure alignment throughout the organization.
- **Choose inspiration over bare minimum:** Prioritize inspiration over compliance when crafting purpose statements. Purpose should go beyond meeting minimum standards and inspire stakeholders to action.
- **Continually reflect:** Continually reflect on your purpose and its alignment with your personal values and aspirations. Use this reflection as an opportunity to refine and strengthen your company's direction and impact.

Books or Articles to Consider

- "Creating Shared Value" by Michael Porter and Mark Kramer
- *Let My People Go Surfing* by Yvon Chouinard

- *The Purpose Driven Life* by Rick Warren
- *The Advantage* by Patrick Lencioni

Tools to Consider
- 1% for the Planet (onepercentfortheplanet.org)
- B Corp (bcorporation.net)

Scale Passion Resources
- Exponential Purpose Workshop: a guided approach to connecting your personal purpose to your corporate one

Find a comprehensive list of resources at ScalePassion.com/Resources.

Chapter 8

Key #2: Drive Clarity

B ack in my YPO days, I used to offer tours of the MegaFood facility in New Hampshire to my fellow CEOs. During the tours, we'd stop and have friendly chats with members of my team who were busily making supplements out of fruits and vegetables from our farming partners. Without my even having to ask them or prompt them, the team members would volunteer to tell a core value story that related to their job, or a purpose story that explained what was the most important thing about what they were doing at that moment.

The YPO visitors would be blown away by the level of strategic awareness that permeated our organization. Most frontline workers in manufacturing companies can probably tell you what they do and how they do it, but few can tell you *why* they do it, much less why the brand is important and unique in their marketplace. All I could do was assure my visitors that it wasn't an accident: we're not in the business of employing drones but of building a team who can express our purpose (and their purposes) through our products.

They were able to do this because we made driving strategic clarity a priority. Do you remember the personal flight plan we discussed in the first part of this book? Now that you will be focusing on how you're leading others, you will want to create a corporate version of this plan—let's call it a business flight plan.

Many people think *strategy* is synonymous with *goal setting*. They think it's about cornering a market or selling more. Typically, a business owner carries around a vision and strategy for the company in their head, which serves as the strategy the company will follow without it being articulated clearly and meaningfully to employees. Such an uncommunicated strategy cannot sustain the company beyond the early phases of starting up and certainly not in an adolescent company experiencing rapid growth.

Unlike large companies that can offer their leaders fully developed operating systems that tell them exactly what to do, fast-growing companies will often have to learn on the fly. Gino Wickman, author of *Traction*, is credited with inventing the genre of the EOS—entrepreneurial operating system—to help small and medium businesses refine and build accountability into their processes. Other versions of the EOS have sprouted up through the years. For example, Verne Harnish created the One-Page Strategic Plan that purported to offer a clean and concise way of helping leaders keep track of their company's strategy. After his time at Intel, John Doerr brought OKRs—objectives and key results—to the world as a way to help align leaders and their teams around goals, priorities, and processes to move the business forward.

I know this because at one time or another, I adopted all strategic systems and more. For example, Patrick Lencioni's six strategic questions represented a breakthrough for me while at MegaFood, but they still lacked several of the inputs I valued, such as customers, market, and company strengths and weaknesses, that I felt should inform a strategy. That's where my emphasis on nailing your strategy comes in: these inputs are critical parts of a continuous process of refining your strategy, and your strategy is a crucial element to drive clarity.

Nailing Your Strategy

An effective leader understands the ABZs of prioritization. *A* is knowing where you are now. *Z* is knowing where you want to go. And *B* is the right next step to move you toward *Z*.

The sequence of questions outlined below provides a logical and comprehensive flow for developing a strategic plan that takes ABZ into account—especially in a two-day retreat setting for impact-minded founders and their leadership teams. The flow moves from establishing foundational principles (purpose and mission) to setting long-term aspirations (vision), assessing the current situation, understanding the target market and external environment, solidifying internal culture (values and norms), and finally, focusing on immediate priorities. This progression ensures that foundational elements inform more detailed strategic planning and action steps.

In stage 1, you answered several questions about yourself to nail your personal flight plan or strategy. The process of nailing your business flight plan or strategy involves answering the following eight questions with your leadership team—we call it the Strategic Map:

1. Why do we exist? (Corporate purpose)
2. Who do we serve? (Customers)
3. What do we do? (Mission)
4. Where is this headed? (Vision)
5. What's going on out there? (External view)
6. Where are we today? (Current situation)
7. How do we behave? (Core values, beliefs, and team norms)
8. What's most important right now? (OKRs)

This refined flow enhances strategic alignment by ensuring that each step builds upon the insights and decisions of the previous ones, creating a coherent and integrated strategic plan. It also places a stronger emphasis on understanding and responding to the market and external environment before deep diving into internal analysis and planning, which can help ensure the strategy is competitive and market driven.

Ending with a focus on immediate priorities and actionable plans ensures the retreat concludes with a clear sense of direction and next steps, setting the stage for effective implementation after the retreat.

To put a little bit of meat on the bones of this outline and illustrate the scope of their influence on your strategy, let's review each step.

1. Why Do We Exist? (Corporate Purpose)

This question drills down to the very heart of the organization's reason for being, beyond making a profit. It's about identifying the broader impact the company aims to have on society, communities, or the environment. A clear corporate purpose is motivational and can guide decision-making at every level. We went deep on how to navigate the development of a corporate purpose in chapter 7.

2. Who Do We Serve? (Customers)

Identifying the target customer, understanding their pain points, and examining how they currently address those needs ensures that the company's offerings remain customer-centric. This insight guides product development, marketing, and sales strategies.

Whether you sell a product or service, who is buying your offer? Where does the customer go to solve the problem? Prioritize them and include cost in your considerations. What are your customers' values, beliefs, and habits? Know these so well that you feel you can give your customer a name. At my former company, we created an avatar named

Vibrant Vanessa who embodied the active, spiritual, health-conscious customer we sought.

Kevin Kelly helped found *Wired* magazine back in 1993. *Wired* won the prestigious National Magazine Award for General Excellence twice (in 1994 and 1997) during Kelly's tenure as executive editor. Since then, he's started companies and nonprofits and written prophetically and brilliantly about business, technology, and society. In 2008, he wrote an essay about the 1,000 True Fans concept that he has refined and that still holds true today.

Kelly explains that a true fan will buy anything you produce. In the article "1,000 True Fans" on his website *The Technium*, Kelly writes: "These diehard fans will drive 200 miles to see you sing; they will buy the hardback and paperback and audible versions of your book; they will purchase your next figurine sight unseen; they will pay for the 'best-of' DVD version of your free YouTube channel; they will come to your chef's table once a month." If you can acquire something in the neighborhood of a thousand true fans like this, "you can make a living."

Creating a clear view of your customer, naming them, and detailing their persona is so important.

3. What Do We Do? (Mission)

A great mission simplifies and clarifies the organization's core activities and offerings. It ensures that everyone inside and outside the organization understands what the company does and stands for, creating a unified direction.

Begin by embracing the principles of simplicity and clarity. Your mission statement should be straightforward and easily understandable to anyone, regardless of their familiarity with your industry. Strip away the complexities and jargon, and focus on articulating the core essence of your business in plain language. Resist the temptation to embellish or make your statement overly broad. Specificity is key. Your mission statement should differentiate your company from its competitors by reflecting the unique value or approach you bring to the market. It should capture the essence of what your company genuinely does on a day-to-day basis to serve its customers.

Internally, your mission statement serves as a compass, guiding decision-making and prioritization. Externally, your mission statement provides a clear and concise way to communicate your company's purpose to customers, clients, and other stakeholders. It clarifies your value proposition and attracts the right customers who resonate with your mission.

Ultimately, your mission statement forms the foundation for your strategic planning efforts. It acts as a grounding point, ensuring that all initiatives and efforts are aligned with the core of what your company does. Take the time to craft a mission statement that accurately reflects your company's identity and purpose, and use it as a guiding light in shaping your strategy and driving your business forward.

4. Where Is This Headed? (Vision)

This forward-looking question defines the aspirational future of the company. Setting a vision, along with long-term goals like BHAGs, provides direction and inspires stakeholders to strive toward a common future.

Understanding the concept of a vision is essential for any company seeking long-term success. A vision articulates where the company is headed and provides a clear picture of the desired future state. It serves as a beacon, guiding strategic decisions and inspiring action among employees and stakeholders. To develop a compelling vision for your company, start by envisioning the future you want to create. Imagine what success looks like on a grand scale, beyond incremental improvements, and aim for transformational change.

One approach to developing a vision is inspired by Dan Sullivan's 10x thinking and Jim Collins's BHAG. Think big and aim for a vision that is 10 times greater than your current reality. Consider what your company could achieve if there were no limitations or constraints. What bold, audacious goal could propel your organization to new heights? Engage your team in brainstorming sessions to generate ideas and explore possibilities. Encourage creativity and innovation, and be willing to challenge conventional thinking.

Once you've identified potential visions, evaluate them based on their alignment with your company's purpose, values, mission, and long-term objectives. Choose a vision that resonates with your team and inspires passion and commitment. Remember that a compelling vision should be ambitious yet achievable, challenging yet realistic. It should stretch your organization beyond its comfort zone while instilling confidence in its attainability.

Ensure that every member of your team understands and embraces the vision, and empower them to contribute to its realization. A shared vision unites your organization behind a common purpose and provides a road map for success in the years to come. By investing time and effort into developing a compelling vision, you lay the foundation for a future filled with growth, innovation, and impact.

5. What's Going On Out There? (External View)

Analyzing market conditions, competition, and trends is crucial for positioning the company effectively. It helps identify opportunities for innovation and differentiation.

Understanding the environment in which you operate your business is vital. Who out there is trying to solve the same thing you are? What are the major trends affecting your customers' choices? Have you thought about the pace of change out there? What steps are you taking, or can you take, to get out in front of the change? Staying on top of your marketplace takes consistent effort. It's not like an annual checkup.

When studying your competition, don't limit yourself to direct competitors. Access syndicated data or research, such as SPINS, Nielsen, or other industry-specific reports, to give you a broader picture of your category. In addition to understanding your competition and analyzing market trends, stay abreast of emerging trends that could impact your business. Trends can arise from various sources, including technological advancements, changes in consumer behavior, shifts in regulatory landscapes, and global events.

As the CEO of MegaFood, I was keenly aware of the growing convergence between technology and wellness. This intersection presented both opportunities and challenges for our industry, as innovations such as at-home testing kits had the potential to reshape the way consumers approached their health and wellness routines. By tracking these trends closely, we were able to anticipate changes in consumer preferences and adapt our product offerings and marketing strategies accordingly.

Remember, the marketplace is constantly evolving, so it's essential to remain agile and adaptable in your approach to strategy and decision-making.

6. Where Are We Today? (Current Situation)

Before diving into objective setting, you need to gain a clear understanding of the current internal and external situation of the company. This involves assessing key performance indicators (KPIs), conducting a SWOT analysis (strengths, weaknesses, opportunities, threats), evaluating your team, and mapping out pain points within the organization. This process serves as a realistic starting point for objective setting by providing insights into both the areas of strength to leverage and the challenges to address.

Delve deeply into your financial situation by asking what your revenue streams, profit margins, and cash flow are like right now. Go a step further and project these metrics into the future—where do you expect to be in 6 months, 12 months, and 5 years? By forecasting your financial trajectory, you can identify potential areas for growth, investment, or cost reduction, ensuring that your strategic objectives are financially viable and aligned with your long-term goals.

7. How Do We Behave? (Core Values, Beliefs, and Team Norms)

Writer and management consultant Peter Drucker famously did not write that "culture eats strategy for breakfast." But in a March 28, 1991, article called "The Coming of the New Organization," what Drucker *did* say was that "culture—no matter how defined—is singularly persistent." (It's not hard to see why the slicker truism wiggled its way into business lore!) In either case, he didn't mean that strategy didn't matter but rather that culture mattered more than people generally thought. What values, norms, and behaviors define your company culture? How do these elements contribute to or hinder your ability to achieve your objectives? Understanding the cultural dynamics within the organization enables us to leverage our strengths and address any cultural challenges that may impede our progress.

Establishing core values and team norms shapes the company's culture, influencing how team members interact with each other and with stakeholders. A strong, positive culture enhances team cohesion, productivity, and overall company reputation.

Core values are often confused with beliefs, but there are important differences that should guide your use of them. Core values are the fundamental principles and ethical standards that guide an organization's behaviors, decisions, and actions. When core values are used as criteria for hiring, it's beneficial to frame them in a way that describes the character and behaviors of potential team members. This approach helps in assessing whether candidates' values align with those of the organization.

Beliefs are the convictions or accepted truths that an organization holds. They are assumptions or interpretations that guide the understanding of the world and the organization's place in it. Beliefs are important because they shape the worldview of the organization and its strategic direction. Beliefs such as "people are our greatest asset," "ethical practices lead to sustainable success," and "diversity drives innovation" underpin the rationale for why things are done a certain way within a company.

In essence, core values are what an organization upholds as its standards for action and behavior, while beliefs are the underlying convictions that provide context and meaning to these values. Both are crucial in defining an organization's culture and guiding its strategy and operations.

A third element is team norms, which describe the specific expectations and rules that govern how a team operates and interacts on a day-to-day basis. While core values and beliefs are broad and shape the organization's overall culture and strategy, team norms are more focused and practical, directly influencing how team members work together. Regular meeting schedules, response time for emails, decision-making processes, and communication styles are all examples of team norms.

8. What's Most Important Right Now? (OKRs)

"Given all this, what's most important, right now?" This is how I lead this section in a two-day retreat. I literally go back and read the entire flight plan, starting with "Why do we exist?" all the way through "How do we behave?" Once the team has aligned around and absorbed the flight plan up to this point, I simply ask, "Given all this, what's most important right now?" And then we brainstorm, organize, and prioritize the answers into clear objectives and key results.

Setting short-term OKRs and ensuring clear communication

throughout the organization helps maintain focus on what needs immediate attention. Then, identifying critical success factors needed to accomplish these OKRs enables the company to allocate resources efficiently and effectively.

Answering these eight questions quarterly in a strategic, off-site retreat is paramount to driving clarity. Consistently, I see business owners who try to skip directly to this step get off track and sideways.

Listen to Your F-bomb, Grasshopper

I'm seeing a lot of pressure on the companies that I work with around growth. Usually, the pressure is coming from the business owners themselves to lock into this investment model or that one. Such models are predicated on achieving growth through higher levels of monthly sales or revenues. Growth is critical to your company's health and impact. Growth will help you achieve your vision and fulfill your mission. But growth is better understood as a by-product of purpose rather than the purpose itself. Lately, I've had to remind leaders that their purpose has practically nothing to do with growth. Their purpose has everything to do with improving the world.

Bear with me here because this observation connects back to your business flight plan—particularly to clarity. I would submit that when a business owner or the investors around a business owner get focused on growth at all cost, the company starts making sacrifices that can damage morale, the product you put out into the market, and your relationship with the customers who fell in love with your company because of your real purpose.

And sometimes that damage can be irreversible.

How will you know you are so busy doing "what" you and your investors think you have to do to grow that you forget "why" you got into this business in the first place? At some point, you'll pick your head up and say either to yourself or a trusted colleague, "What the f*ck are we doing?" It's a rhetorical question, really, one that stems from doing too much of the what and too little of the why. Your F-bomb, or whatever exclamation you make, will be proof that you are feeling out of integrity with your purpose and that realignment is needed.

As Kwai Chang Caine's master would have said in a Kung Fu parallel universe, "Listen to your F-bomb, Grasshopper." (Those of a certain age will know the iconic television series *Kung Fu*.)

Succumbing to the pressure for growth is based on the fallacy that purpose is a "nice to have" but not "need to have" part of your business. Most studies I'm familiar with have shown that purpose-driven companies have more intrinsic value and receive higher valuations from private equity investors than non-purpose-driven companies. One such study, a biennial report titled "Global Sustainable Investment Review" from the Global Sustainable Investment Alliance (GSIA), has consistently shown a rising trend in sustainable investing, indicating that companies focusing on social impact are more valuable to investors or the big strategic firms.

Cutting corners on product quality, team development, and customer education—to use obvious examples—does brands and their investors no great favor.

Go back to your flight plan. Remind yourself why you exist, who you serve, how your team members behave toward one another and toward your customers, and what you need to do right now to change the world one customer at a time. That's where your strategic focus should always remain, even in and, perhaps, especially in, a time when so much of our daily lives is focused on what's broken.

If you don't have a business flight plan or "why we exist" statement at your company, *do not pass go*. Instead, devote your next meeting to creating one. I suggest spending two days focused on this per quarter (more on that in chapters 9 and 10, so read on!).

Focus on using your business to make the world a better place, and the world will likely want more of what you have to offer. As respected entrepreneurial coach Dan Sullivan has said, too many business owners focus on "the gap" between expected and actual earnings or revenues, as though these figures were the real goal of the business. You're going to be up some quarters and down others, but these up and down figures are the *results*, not the goals. The goal is your purpose: "to make the world a better place through scalable, fault-tolerant, distributable databases with ACID transactions"—sorry, had to throw that one back in there.

The point is that if you're a business leader, it feels rotten to miss your financial targets, but the answer is not found in the outputs of your plan but rather in the plan itself. What did Shakespeare write—"The play's the thing"? Well, the plan's the thing too. Your plan is what gets you to your desired outcome, not shifting your expected outcome. Proper planning looks forward, backward, and to the present. The next time you feel the vertigo of ups and downs, take a deep breath and follow these five steps:

1. **Make time for your quarterly retreats:** That's a retreat every three months in which you take a day or two to step back from working *in* your business to work *on* your business. Closely follow the Strategic Map questions highlighted earlier.

2. **Re-examine your customer:** Are they buying in a new place or in a new way? Have they given you feedback that could suggest ways you might do something new or different?

3. **Ask yourself about your market:** Are there new trends or competitors on the scene that have changed the game for you? Is someone undercutting you? Is there a trend you might seize and integrate into your products or services?

4. **Systematize your data and bring it to your retreat:** Don't panic and react to every little upward and downward spike on a daily or weekly basis. You are much more likely to make sound decisions

with more data and more brains around the table to interpret them, so be patient and make this a discussion point at your next strategic meeting.

5. **Revisit your why and determine what's most important right now as a priority:** The sales or revenue goals should come at the end of proper planning, not the beginning.

The big questions often revolve around your objectives and key results. Focus on these in support of your purpose, and your financial goals will fall into place. And if they don't, train your sights on learning where you're missing your marks. When you focus on learning, you'll find yourself being less emotionally swayed whether you meet, exceed, or miss your numbers. This will lead to better decision-making across the board.

So don't let the financial-goal tail wag the strategic-plan dog. Those monthly revenue figures will never go up exactly like the investment models forecast them to, but you will learn to celebrate the lessons and the victories in your journey—a journey that is a marathon and not a sprint.

Lew's Tips & Resources

Dad would say that if you are going to do it right, you're going to need a plan. Clarity starts and ends with a plan that your team is inspired by and can commit to.

Maxim 1: Make a Difference

- **Why do we exist? (corporate purpose):** Defining the corporate purpose beyond profit ensures that the organization's efforts are directed toward making a positive impact on society, communities, or the environment.
- **Who do we serve? (customers):** Identifying and understanding the target customer allows the company to tailor its offerings to meet their needs effectively. Note: most companies target too broad a market—narrow it down for more clarity and focus.
- **What do we do? (mission):** A clear mission statement communicates the core activities and offerings of the organization, guiding decision-making and aligning stakeholders around a common direction.
- **Where is this headed? (vision):** Setting a bold and compelling vision inspires stakeholders to strive toward a common future and provides direction for long-term strategic planning.

Maxim 2: Be Bold

- **Nail your strategy:** Emphasize the importance of continuously refining strategy based on critical inputs such as customer insights, market analysis, and internal capabilities.
- **How do we behave? (core values and team norms):** Establishing core values, beliefs, and team norms shapes the organization's

culture, influencing behavior and interactions among team members.

- **Listen to your F-bomb:** Remind business owners to stay true to the organization's purpose and values, even amid pressure for growth, to maintain integrity and long-term sustainability.

Maxim 3: Do It Right

- **Drive clarity:** Making strategic clarity a priority ensures that employees understand not only what they do and how they do it but also why their work matters within the broader context of the organization's purpose and vision.
- **What's most important right now?** Setting short-term objectives and key results (OKRs) ensures that the organization remains focused on what needs immediate attention and allocates resources effectively to achieve its goals.
- **Cascade clarity:** Recognize the positive impact of clarity on employee engagement, performance, and productivity across all levels of the organization.

Books or Articles to Consider

- *1,000 True Fans* by Kevin Kelly
- *Traction* by Gino Wickman
- *Scaling Up* by Verne Harnish
- *The Advantage* by Patrick Lencioni

Scale Passion Resources

- "Running a Retreat Workshop": a guided approach to running a two-day strategic retreat
- "Developing Core Values Workshop": a guided approach to developing corporate core values

- "Sample Customer Personas and Descriptions": a simple selection of sample customer personas for inspiration
- "Sample Answers to Strategic Map Questions": gain inspiration from this selection of answers to all the key questions needed to drive clarity

Find a comprehensive list of resources at ScalePassion.com/Resources.

Chapter 9

Key #3: Constantly Pursue Alignment

I was consulting with a set of cofounders who had launched a successful company that was rapidly scaling from $1 million a month to triple that within the next year. We were beginning a two-day retreat, a point where I usually dig deep into the founders' goals for the business.

When I asked the founder, whom I'll call Joe, what he wanted, he spoke passionately for 15 minutes about his dream of building the company to give to his children. Then I asked his cofounder, "Carl," the same question, and he enthusiastically explained that he wanted to build the company over the next three to five years, then sell it so he would have the funds to start another company.

Both worthy goals, but not aligned. We spent the next two days working to get the cofounders aligned. We succeeded by negotiating Joe's buyout of Carl over the next three to five years. But can you imagine the headaches that would have ensued had they continued forward as cofounders who were completely out of alignment? Joe would be more than willing to spend a million dollars on enterprise resource planning software because he would be thinking 20 to 30 years out, and Carl would want to make sure they kept as much profit as possible to maximize valuation at the end of five years.

It would have been a bad time for all.

Alignment plays a huge role in scaling passion. First and foremost, alignment describes the state in which two or more founders find themselves when they are on the same wavelength about why they want to launch a company and where they want it to go. An aligned organization is one in which the founders or CEOs and their leadership teams are aligned on their business flight plan. An aligned team can make magic happen. Only by achieving alignment can the company's purpose scale to every corner of the larger team.

In this chapter, we will look at the three steps you have to take to build a leadership team that is aligned and thus able to serve as the foundation for building a purpose-driven company.

The three steps are:

1. Getting the team right
2. Building trust
3. Constantly communicating

Getting the Team Right

I have a friend who started a fast-growing, successful company. I'll call her Lisa. A while back, she invited me to visit her company and offer her some advice. Lisa was feeling frustrated because her company was going gangbusters and had attracted interest from what can only be described as the holy grail of customers for her particular line of products: Target.

Getting into the Targets of this world used to seem like a dream, but once Target started returning her calls, it felt like a lot of pressure. On the one hand, her company stood to grow from $14 million to $40 million and become a major player in her marketplace. On the other hand, failing to make the leap, she felt, would consign her company to irrelevance. To compound the pressure she felt, Target was asking for a big honking plan, complete with her vision, an analysis of her supply chain, and an outline for a three-year pipeline of new products.

Lisa didn't know how to provide any of this. And that's when she realized, "Oh my god, my leadership team can't help me with this, either."

Her COO, let's call him Bryson, had been with her from the beginning. He had built amazing relationships with key suppliers, and there was basically no problem he couldn't troubleshoot with a phone call. But now Lisa needed something other than a go-to guy; she needed somebody who could tell her what needed to be done next year and three years out to meet their goals—what kind of investment in technology and equipment will be needed, who to hire when, and so on.

She had to admit that four out of six of her leaders probably needed to be replaced, not because they were bad people or bad at their jobs, but simply because the company had outgrown them.

Those were hard conversations she didn't want to have! And so Lisa felt trapped. After all, she loved her team. She'd handpicked them, and since then, they had bought in to her vision and supported her every decision with passionate loyalty and creativity. *Wait a minute*, Lisa thought. *That's the problem, isn't it? I've hired followers rather than leaders.*

The leadership qualities she valued before, such as creativity and energy and resourcefulness, weren't the strategic thinking or experience she needed to move the company forward.

She thought about the Monday morning meeting when, surrounded by her top six doers, Lisa fielded their problems and solved each and every one of them. When the company had 10 and then 20 people, this was doable. Now with 60 people, there were simply too many issues for her to handle.

"Congratulations, Lisa," I said to her after she related this thinking to me. "You've made the first crucial insight a business owner needs to have: get the right butts in the seats."

Whether you are a founder or CEO of a small, medium, or large company, or even a leader leading a department within a company, alignment is a key criterion for scaling your passion. It all begins with your team. I have found there are three main reasons that business owners and their teams fail to align.

The first, as Lisa learned, is not having the right people in the room or, as Jim Collins said in *Good to Great*, not having the right people on the bus in the right seats. As the business owner, your first order of business ought to be assessing your leadership team—not simply for skill set or experience but also for their comfort levels on what I call the leadership continuum.

The continuum implies that all of us have more or less the ability or *inclination* to be a leader and that, the further out in time you are comfortable thinking and performing, the greater capacity you have for strategy or vision. Not everybody can be a visionary; companies need people whose sweet spots fall all along the spectrum, from tactical to managerial to directorial to strategic and visionary.

But, as you'll see from figure 1, entrepreneurial or fast-growth environments tend to compress the timelines for everybody, leaving little time or brainpower for longer-term planning. This happens because small entrepreneur-led companies often carry too many vice presidents who are rewarded for their loyalty and good work rather than their ability to be strategic. The more strategic the role in the company, the further out ahead you need to think. Fast-growth companies often lose sight of this because of an all-hands-on-deck mindset and the business owner's intense investment in the company.

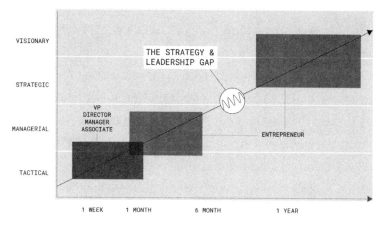

Figure 1: The leadership continuum:
the entrepreneur or solo leader runs the business.

The problem arises when promotions effectively take leaders out of their sweet spots, which may involve a more tactical, day-to-day focus. The fancy title doesn't match what they do, their personal sweet spot, or what their expectations are day in and day out. In these cases, I sometimes show leaders figure 2 and ask them to point to where they feel most comfortable. More often than not, if they are being honest, they indicate a spot below their title.

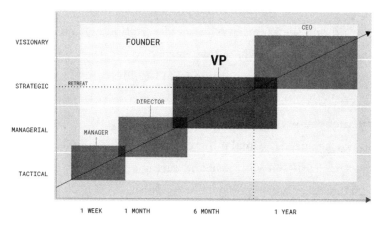

Figure 2: The leadership continuum: the scaling business.

When I took the reins at my previous company, I spent the better part of a year hiring new vice presidents and reassigning the current ones to positions more in line with their sweet spots or assisting them in finding another opportunity. Only then could we begin to set and implement a strategy to meet the company's ambitious growth targets. All in all, it took three years, but we did end up looking like figure 2, with 90% of our leaders properly titled and operating in a manner consistent with their abilities.

Getting leaders in their sweet spots is so important for the business owner wishing to drive strategy at any size company. The key to building strategic alignment begins with the hiring process, which includes not only bringing new talent into your organization but also reassigning or parting ways with those who don't fit the organization's needs. When I was building out my senior leadership teams, I often showed internal candidates actual job descriptions of vice presidents at more mature companies so they could see the kind of knowledge, skills, and experience required for these positions. A vice president of operations for a mature company, for example, might call for 10 years of experience running a two-hundred-person team and leading the acquisition and integration of new technologies and facilities.

If they matched up, I would be the first one to applaud them and consider them candidates for the revamped vice presidency. About 90% of the time, they didn't see themselves in the description and quickly realized they were nowhere near where they needed to be. Then I either worked with them to move into new positions that would report to the new leader, or we parted ways.

Whether you reassign or part ways with a member of your team, the business owner needs to make the conversation about them, delivering the message clearly but with love and caring and in the full expectation that your coworker will experience, at the very least if reassignment is the route, disappointment. And if letting go is the route, you can expect them to go through phases of shock, anger, fear, and sadness (not necessarily in that order) that need to be processed.

Understand that everything after, "I am truly sorry about this, but I have to let you go," will not be heard. Things like terms of the dismissal should be emailed to them in clear, simple language, as trying to talk them through them rarely works. Give them time to process their feelings, even if it means arranging to circle back after the weekend to finalize some details.

You'll also need to process your own feelings. I recommend processing your feelings with someone other than the person being let go before you have the conversation.

Here is a quick rundown of the way I advise business owners to approach difficult conversations:

1. Stay calm and clear. Instead of focusing on the details during the conversation, plan to send the next steps and termination details in writing.
2. Make the discussion about them, not you. They are the ones being let go; how sad you feel about the situation is not relevant to them at this moment.
3. Give them lots of "oxygen"—space and time—to feel their emotions and work through them.
4. Do all you can to support them in their next steps.
5. Process your own feelings with a trusted friend/advisor (not with the person being let go).

In the end, the termination is about your friend, colleague, and teammate in that moment. It's not about you.

Building Trust

Once you get the right people in the room, they will have to develop trust. Trust is necessary in order for people to practice candor, and candor is necessary in order for people to achieve alignment. For example, you can put a great executive team in place, but they still report to you, the business owner, so if at the conclusion of a presentation in which you fiercely scribbled out a year's worth of priorities on the whiteboard you receive not a hint of pushback or questioning from your team, it means they don't trust you enough to disagree with you.

Ditto for their interactions with each other. If none of them can disagree and debate a point without descending to awkward silence or rage, you do not have a trusting team in place.

I learned from my work with the Conscious Leadership Group several ways to build trust within your team. The first way involves taking 100% responsibility for your thoughts and feelings. As we explored earlier, conscious leadership distinguishes between the "below the line" mindset where things happen *to* us and we are primarily concerned with being right, and an "above the line" mindset where things are happening *by* us and we are motivated by curiosity. When we are curious, we are more likely to be in integrity because nothing—thoughts, feelings, beliefs, opinions—is out of bounds as a topic for scrutiny. We acknowledge them, and we deal with them.

Second, it's common for all of us to build up stories in our heads about what others are thinking or feeling. An exercise called "Fact Versus Story" might help you move past these stories and ground your discussions in facts. The point of this exercise isn't to win points but to clear the air of false narratives.

The business owners I know are big storytellers. Their stories are about knowing exactly what the customer wants, having the perfectly designed and conceived product, lamenting employees who don't know what they're doing, and not wasting time trying something that didn't work before.

But these aren't facts or even reasons or arguments. They're the stories the brain contrives to keep us safe, part of the fight or flight mechanism we employ unconsciously to protect our self-esteem and will to carry on.

The problem arises when the story doesn't keep us safe but risks exposing worse problems, such as an unaligned leadership team whose members regret the day they left their previous jobs to join our company!

Recognize when you're telling a story. The easiest way to do that is to capture the facts. The facts of a situation are anything that a video camera might record, for example. If we look at QuickBooks and see that our revenue is up 10% compared to the previous month, we are registering a fact. However, if we assume that revenue is up because employees worked harder, we have made up a story about the figure. If an employee regularly shows up five minutes after a meeting start time, that can be a fact. However, if we conclude that the employee is bad and doesn't respect the leader, we have made up a story about them.

Do you see how distinguishing stories from facts changes *everything*? By listing out the facts of any topic or issue about which you are meeting or having a discussion, you insert a little gap between stimulus and response. Putting this space between the fact of your tardy employee and the story of their threat to your authority will allow you to ask them, after a meeting, why they have shown up late—and to do so with genuine curiosity!

A similar dynamic can take place when you receive customer feedback. In the heat of the moment, you might interpret their constructive criticism as a sign they hate your product. But you couldn't know this unless you asked them, and they told you that, right? And, in the meantime, you might be discounting excellent advice.

When you separate fact from story, you get different interpretations—some positive, some negative—of the same set of facts. The savvy founder will establish a solid framework of facts before allowing the team to begin constructing a story around them. I have found that one of the best ways to do this is to set aside ample time at your quarterly retreats to review the facts around marketplace data, new consumer research, financials, and so on. Then, at your monthly strategy meetings, review the key performance indicators you're tracking to be sure you separate the story you're making up about your company from the truth.

The third principle of conscious leadership you can use for alignment involves speaking unarguably. There's an expression called "poking the baby," which refers to saying something about a child that the parent might find offensive, such as commenting on the child's physical appearance or behavior in almost any other way than complimentary. When applied to business, the obvious problem arises when those to whom the founder looks to help her build the business are afraid of speaking their minds for fear of, yes, poking the baby.

I've heard exasperated business owners exclaim, "Why didn't you tell me that before?" to employees, cofounders, or other stakeholders. Sometimes these folks had tried to voice their opinions, only to be ignored or unheard by the founder. But more often, they held their criticisms or opposition in check out of fear of angering the founder, who did little or nothing to encourage candor.

I've sat in meetings in which a founder was expounding a grand vision and felt myself getting a little queasy. My head would start hurting, my neck might tense up, or I'd feel a knot in my stomach as I listened to something that wasn't making sense.

What to do?

Speaking unarguably is a way to give your emotions their day in court, but doing so in productive rather than divisive ways—effectively turning your thoughts and feelings into facts. The easiest form of speaking unarguably is describing your thoughts in the moment.

"I'm having a thought that if we go ahead and try this, then XYZ will happen."

Or, "I'm wondering if what you are talking about is similar to what we tried back in 2015, where we did XYZ with this result?"

Notice how you are not challenging the other person's credibility or intelligence; instead, you're describing thoughts that have popped into your head. They may be true or false, but they are not debatable *because they're yours.*

You can do the same thing with feelings, although this one is a bit harder because emotions are often harder to share than thoughts. You might say, "I'm feeling afraid, and I'm making up the story that the same thing that happened to me five years ago is going to happen now." Admitting that you are experiencing fear will make somebody feel closer to you and want to listen, and once again, your emotion is unarguable because it's yours.

I once led a retreat for a company and noticed that things had become tense between the founder and his team. Gradually, the founder admitted to feeling "frustrated" by the pushback he felt from his team, triggering his emotions, which led to a bit of a rant right before he shut down. When I polled the room of leaders and asked what primary emotion (anger, fear, sadness, joy, creative) the founder was experiencing, everyone said "anger." When I asked the founder to clarify, he said his primary emotion was not anger but fear of not being a successful leader. This admission produced an immediate softening effect on his team and allowed the founder to dispel the erroneous narrative that had been swirling around in his (and the team's) head!

Another way of speaking unarguably is describing a physical sensation associated with emotion. This one probably takes the most practice and involves evoking our understanding that sometimes our bodies tell us something before our brain can process it. That knot in your stomach or pounding in your head may be giving you a heads-up that you need to speak up—and the sooner, the better. While you wouldn't say, "Your ideas are making me sick to my stomach," you might very well say, "I'm feeling a knot in my stomach hearing you talk about XYZ."

Can't argue with that.

Sometimes if you just allow that to come out in the meeting, people will want to understand why and give you the space to really explore that feeling. This type of teammate support is a real game changer when it comes to alignment.

These approaches can strip away the drama and accusatory behaviors that undermine trust, cutting off conversation and problem-solving. The alternative—not finding a productive way through core emotions and drama—can lead to more or less permanent divisions in which what is left unsaid in the meeting appears in more toxic forms outside the meeting.

Speaking unarguably when you're at retreats, or even when you're just thinking out loud and brainstorming, is a great way to bring a team closer and soften the perceived threats of disagreement. The key in all these techniques is to approach discussions and challenges in the spirit of curiosity rather than in the desire to be right; only then will your team feel the kind of common ground they need among one another to be candid about their thoughts and feelings, knowing that these are in service of working toward a common solution rather than defending an individual position.

And then, once you've established this level of trust, I put great stock in Jeff Bezos's classic five-step process for achieving alignment and turning a meeting into concrete, actionable plans. They are:

1. **Propose:** Present the problem or solution. Invite team members to ask clarifying questions.
2. **Question and disagree:** Debate the problem or solution. Disagreements must be supported by evidence, data, experience, or examples.
3. **Decide:** The team makes or ratifies a decision.
4. **Commit:** Everyone, regardless of their initial stance, commits to successfully executing the decision.
5. **Implement:** The team works together on implementation, monitoring roadblocks, and iterating as needed.

Constantly Communicating

The rules of engagement—*how* you and your team behave with each other to build trust and communicate effectively—are critical to alignment. But there is another contributor to alignment that is important: communication.

As the leader, you are responsible for ensuring that the business understands your flight plan in the deepest possible way. This includes finding opportunities to mention the purpose, mission, core values, and major priorities of the company as often as possible. Here are a few approaches to ensure that you are taking responsibility for and delivering on this imperative.

First, read a shortened version of the flight plan in every group meeting. The only exception might be a daily huddle. Second, find opportunities to celebrate when the company or people in the company do something great that expresses your purpose or core values. At MegaFood, we had a Culture Club Committee that nominated people who expressed a core value to be recognized at our quarterly town hall.

Third, use your phone to record a voice memo and send it to the whole company. I used to do this each Monday during my drive into the office. The memo only has to be three to five minutes long. I might talk about a great encounter I had with a customer while visiting with a field sales rep, or I might tell everyone how excited I was about the upcoming town hall and the opportunity to share some inspirational stories with them from my travels. Always bring the message in some way back to the company's purpose.

Lastly, if you have key stakeholders, such as a board or investors, make it a habit to communicate with them at least every other week. I would schedule this investor communication in my calendar on a Friday and take some time to express what had me excited, what kept me up at night, and what my top priorities were—as well as how those stakeholders could help.

I always led these communications with a brief synopsis of the flight plan and where we were against our OKRs. But I never failed to mention our purpose and our core values along with the OKRs for this key constituency. The importance of proactive communication cannot be overstated.

Lew's Tips & Resources

Lew Craven was well respected by his tribe. He was in his sweet spot, operated with integrity, and stayed on purpose. He would understand the value of aligning with like-minded people to support one another, provide encouragement, and drive impact.

Maxim 1: Make a Difference

- **Alignment with purpose:** Founders and leadership teams must be aligned on the company's purpose and vision for scaling.
- **Right people in the right roles:** It's crucial to have the right people in leadership positions who can contribute strategically to the company's growth and vision.
- **Building trust:** Trust among team members is essential for fostering candid discussions, which lead to alignment and effective decision-making.

Maxim 2: Be Bold

- **Re-evaluate leadership:** Business owners must be willing to reassess the capabilities of their team members and make tough decisions about reassigning or letting go individuals who no longer fit the organization's needs.
- **Embrace difficult conversations:** Business owners should approach difficult conversations with empathy and clarity, focusing on supporting the individual being affected while also processing their own emotions with a trusted advisor.
- **Speak unarguably:** Encourage team members to express their thoughts and feelings in a productive manner, focusing on facts

and personal experiences rather than engaging in accusatory or confrontational behaviors.

Maxim 3: Do It Right

- **Jeff Bezos's alignment process:** Adopt a structured process for achieving alignment and making decisions, emphasizing proposal, questioning, decision-making, commitment, and implementation.
- **Constant communication:** Consistent and transparent communication is essential for ensuring everyone in the organization understands the company's purpose, mission, values, and priorities. Use various channels to reinforce alignment and engagement.

Books or Articles to Consider

- *Good to Great* by James Collins
- *Topgrading* by Bradford Smart
- *Who* by Geoff Smart and Randy Street
- *The 15 Commitments of Conscious Leadership* by Jim Dethmer, Diana Chapman, and Kaley Klemp

Scale Passion Resources

- "Running a Retreat Workshop": a guided approach to running a two-day strategic retreat

Find a comprehensive list of resources at ScalePassion.com/Resources.

Chapter 10

Key #4: Set the Pace

T he concept of synchrony really hit home when I became familiar with the sport of crew. My daughter Emily rowed from junior high school all the way into college at Clemson University. I've watched more than a few of her meets. And to watch a boat of eight rowers with a coxswain swinging and rolling through the water is a beautiful picture of harmony and fusion among teammates that makes you forget to focus on your own child and lose yourself in the rhythm—indeed, the synchrony— that propels the boat.

You don't think about how hard each person rows because, try as you might, you can't isolate one person from the others!

This is not to say that each rower doesn't have her own strengths and role to play. Some focus on balancing the boat, others on direction, and still others on power. In other words, they aren't all just straining at the oar! They are doing different things but doing them in absolute synchrony with each other.

If a boat full of rowers comes out of the gate at full sprint and hopes to maintain that pace for two thousand meters, they've got another thing coming. My daughter would be the first to admit that coming out too fast is the fastest way to end your race early.

The same thing holds true for leading your team. This can be hard for business owners to see. As a business owner, you see yourself as a problem-solver who has all the answers and, often, as the proverbial "smartest person in the room." You're often the quickest at thinking and see everything as your responsibility and urgent. If you've built a company from scratch, one hard-won client at a time, and felt the personal pain of losing some along the way, you've developed an obsession with keeping the client happy, even after you wake up one day and realize you now lead a company with plenty of money and more expertise than ever before.

But guess what? As the leader, you are responsible for maintaining synchrony on the boat that is your business! You are the one who is charged with making sure your team doesn't burn itself out in the first part of the race.

There are times for urgency and putting out fires—we'll get to those a bit later—but when holding quarterly retreats or even monthly meetings with your leadership team, and especially when you've put a new team in place, feed them oxygen.

Take a deep breath. In. Out. There you go. When it comes to leading others and focusing them on behaving consciously with each other and making a difference in the world, I'm a big believer in the power of oxygen. When I refer to the need to give a process or a person "lots of oxygen," I mean lots of presence, patience, space, curiosity, and safety. Oxygen offers an antidote to frenzy and unbridled urgency.

It's about giving the right amount of time to the right things and the right people at the right time.

I often do this by asking various members of the team to read parts of our flight plan out loud to get us in a common frame of mind. What is our purpose? Who is our ideal customer? What do we do? This is seriously grounding material and can be done in just a few minutes. At first, some may think it seems a bit cookie cutter, but eventually they see how it helps make everything we discuss click.

This chapter is largely about the power of meetings. Along the way, I've learned that people tend to take meetings too seriously and overlook opportunities for creative or analytical play, which can be productive. In this chapter, you will learn about the power of presence, that every meeting should have a purpose, and that different meetings have different purposes that should be made clear ahead of meeting time. You'll see that when properly understood and appropriately scheduled with the right people at the table, meetings are one of your most powerful leadership tools.

Establish a Corporate Rhythm

Once you've got your team correctly aligned along the leadership continuum (see chapter 9) and have built a level of comfort and trust, you're ready to establish a rhythm for the business that will enable you to run your company on a daily basis *and* plan for the future.

When I hold my October strategic retreat with my leadership team, I require them to bring in their calendar for the full upcoming year. The goal is to schedule the weekly, monthly, and quarterly team meetings along with quarterly board meetings, town halls, and any other important events that, once scheduled, are set in stone with the expectation that your team schedules their personal time appropriately. I generally implore my team to take at least four weeks off, and this scheduling session allows me to show my own commitment to the pace and to them by signaling to everyone on the team that at certain times of year they will have to slow down, take a deep breath, and be strategic.

As the coxswain of the boat, the one with the megaphone in your hand, you must realize that another benefit to achieving harmony is that it also works to give individuals—the balancers, steering, and power strokers—the opportunity to see where they fit in the company priorities, especially when it comes to identifying what's most important for the boat. For example, if I'm in a marketing meeting as a marketing person and driving sales is the most important priority, I can see that and see where I connect. If I'm an operations-focused person and know that driving sales is number one, I know that we've got to stay in stock! This lifts me out of my daily head-down grind to see where I might be able to help another department that relies on me, or that I rely on.

The leader—the metaphorical coxswain—needs to be the one carrying the megaphone and ensuring that everybody is fulfilling their role and staying in sync. She sets the pace and points out the places where course correction is needed. Maybe the marketplace is cooking up faster than expected and the boat needs to pick up the pace without careening into a riverbank. That's the coxswain's job and the founder's too.

As I've mentioned, one of the ways I keep my team pulling in the same direction is to make a habit of revisiting our flight plan at every meeting. Today, when I lead all the retreats with our current client companies, we read the flight plan first to ensure everybody's still aligned on it. And even when I lead a monthly strategic meeting, we always start with the flight plan. It's a mantra of sorts that we recite to create ease and clarity before diving deep into the particulars.

Maintaining that shared focus, as well as competitive speed and balance, is your job as the leader. And as your company grows, it may be your most important job. That's why you get to hold the megaphone!

Strategic Versus Tactical Meetings

Let's face it, not all meetings are created equal. There's a stark difference between tactical and strategic discussions, and trying to blend them into one can lead to confusion and inefficiency. By all means, have both kinds of meetings—but not at the same time.

A brief autobiographical anecdote will illustrate the point. When I started a CEO gig at one company, I spent the first month observing and learning. Every Monday morning, the founder would assemble his entire team in the meeting room and begin a stream-of-consciousness session. Sometimes he would talk nonstop; other times he would field questions and issue orders. Topics big and small were treated the same, and practically no topic was off topic unless the founder said it was. Delegation was limited to the founder saying, more or less, "You do this. You do that."

A fan of Patrick Lencioni's book *Death by Meeting*, I found myself delighted when the founder and I sat down to discuss governance, and he admitted he didn't want to run the company anymore and wanted me to take over the day-to-day as the CEO. Like many truly purpose-driven business owners, this founder wanted to focus on being his brand's chief evangelist and follow the pathway of innovation to come up with ever newer and more revolutionary products. That was his passion, not integrating systems and processes needed to achieve his great vision—and certainly not running meetings!

But I'm a glutton for processes, so I thought, *Great!* The first thing I did was have everyone in the company read *Death by Meeting*, which argues that unproductive meetings lack structure, purpose, and engagement, leading to disengaged employees and ineffective decision-making processes. Lencioni proposes a solution: a new meeting framework that includes different types of meetings, each serving a specific purpose. These meeting types include the daily check-in, the weekly tactical, the monthly strategic, and the quarterly off-site reviews. Lencioni believes that, by implementing this structured approach to meetings, organizations can transform their meetings into dynamic, efficient, and productive sessions that drive alignment, engagement, and better decision-making.

I have been using this approach for more than 20 years as a CEO and founder and have trained my team and clients to practice it too.

The weekly tactical meeting might seem routine, but it serves a crucial purpose: it supports your *purpose*. It's your chance to touch base, review the past week, and figure out how everyone can support each other in moving things forward. These 45 to 90 minutes are the meat-and-potatoes time you need to keep operations on track. It is very tactical: who's doing what, when, and where.

Strategic thinking demands a different mindset and more time.

This is where the monthly strategic meeting really shines. Scheduled after the financial statements are in, it provides the space to take a step back and approach your business like an external consultant. Unlike the weekly meetings, the monthly session should be three to four hours long. This extended time frame lets you thoroughly examine short- to medium-term strategic matters without the pressure to rush through them.

Of course, the most strategic meeting is the quarterly retreat, where you and your leadership team gather to soar to 50 thousand feet and lay in the flight plan that will guide the company into the future. This is a two-day off-site meeting designed to encourage the trust and energy the team needs to have meaningful dialogue (and often debate) to align behind the purpose and lay the track needed to provide clarity for the entire company.

By spreading out your meetings—quarterly retreats with monthly strategics in between and weekly tacticals in between all that—you are removing the rush factor and creating an environment for strategic discussions to breathe—yes, providing more oxygen—thus ensuring that you and your team reach a true alignment. Without this, you might find yourself revisiting the same problems month after month.

Yes, you will always feel pressure to address whatever "hot topic" seems to dominate the office conversation, but as you jot it down on a list of potential subjects for the upcoming monthly meeting, you'll often find that its urgency diminishes by the time the meeting arrives, and yesterday's grenade will likely turn into today's dud.

Agenda?

In general, outside of the strategic retreat, I am not a fan of bringing a fixed agenda to a meeting. If you are operating in a fast-paced environment and solving problems every day, bring the issues that need to be addressed to your monthly or quarterly strategic meetings and spend the first several minutes of the meeting nailing down an agenda based on the most recent data, reports, and challenges. I have found that many of the items we thought needed to be discussed ahead of time were resolved by the time we sat down to talk.

In place of agendas, I recommend bringing a completed CPR—context, purpose, and result—to every meeting. I learned this technique from Jean, the amazing head of marketing I worked with at MegaFood. An example of CPR in practice would go like this:

- **Context:** Several large customers have voiced their displeasure over lower than desired inventories. We're not shipping enough product. Root causes include X, Y, and Z and the key data you need to know is A, B, C. The VP of Operations calls a meeting and invites all those who impact this process.
- **Purpose:** The VP will use the meeting to learn where the breakdowns are occurring in operations and sales and to brainstorm ideas for fixing the problem.
- **Result:** The VP will use the discussion to pull together a smaller group to fix the problem and clarify immediate goals and next steps.

The High-Impact One-on-One

Most of us came of professional age thinking that the most you could expect from a one-on-one with your boss or direct report was personal chat, followed up by a review of what you/they were up to at work. There's nothing wrong with this approach to one-on-ones, but what if you could inject more inspiration into them?

At ScalePassion, we ground our one-on-ones in purpose—the company's purpose, the department's purpose, and the individual purposes of each member of our firm. Think in terms of concentric circles of purpose. As you see how we do it, keep in mind that this process takes all of 10 to 15 minutes tops at the beginning of the sit-down.

First, we ground our meeting in our company's purpose, which at ScalePassion is to radically evolve capitalism. Next, we review the purpose of the department or discipline of our business. If I'm talking to the head of inspiration, for example, Steve Klinetobe, we quickly review how the storytelling purpose of ScalePassion is capturing and articulating the fire and soul of our company and our clients. In my one-on-one with Nick Van Nice, our personal leadership coach, the purpose is to help ScalePassion clients live their personal purpose with integrity and be a positive influence.

Then, we shift to our personal purposes. Nick's personal purpose is to coach leaders to live in their purpose with integrity. Steve's personal purpose is to ignite purpose through storytelling. My personal purpose is scaling impact, both through leaders and through their businesses.

After establishing our purpose, we review personality assessment results, such as the Enneagram assessment or Patrick Lencioni's Working Genius evaluation method, to remind both of us that the person sitting across from us is very likely different from us. The classic question—"Where are we on this?"—will be felt differently by someone who's quick off the starting line versus someone who thrives on detail, and differently still by someone who doesn't respond well to pressure!

Next, we move to OKRs, beginning with personal OKRs—it is absolutely my role as the business owner to understand what my teammate is trying to accomplish personally, especially if it has to do with finding their purpose, energy, focus, and growth mindset. Only then do we talk about business OKRs—those commitments my teammate has made to advance the company's mission and goals.

Again, this takes around 15 minutes. Afterward, I can focus on how I can support them in their work. We spend the rest of the meeting making agreements on what should be done and by whom, and we put all of this in our meeting notes to follow up at the agreed-upon time. This system of one-on-ones creates exceptional continuity over time, but it also allows for continual adjustments on the OKRs.

To get started, don't worry about having everything fully baked. You may not have nailed your and your team's purposes down to the point where you can quickly cover off on them. But the sooner you begin to weave this into your one-on-one meetings, the sooner you will begin to radiate that energy that you need to achieve alignment with, and among, your team.

The beauty of an intentional approach to any meeting is that it moves you away from the default meeting and allows the organizer to purposefully match participants with problem-solving. You can see why I like calling it CPR: building clarity and purpose around your meetings lets you breathe life into them.

The real magic comes in when you apply pace to proactively structure the entire company's schedule. Instead of doing a little of this and a little of that every day, which requires constant shifting from tactical to strategic thinking, think about building out a calendar that allows you to structure your, and your leadership team's, ideal week. Then, schedule project meetings or business development for another day. Designate one day—I typically choose Friday—for "meetless" Friday, allowing for deeper thinking and even more oxygen.

If you get the scheduling down the right way, you can use what you learn from the individual meetings as fodder for the larger group meetings. You will also find that you and your team have more energy and focus throughout the week because they won't be wasting energy constantly shifting gears. In an ideal organization, one-on-ones will feed department meetings while department meetings will feed executive leadership meetings.

A well-paced meeting calendar supports your purpose, drives clarity, allows for trust building, and guides alignment, ensuring that your team is all pulling together in synchrony, like a well-run crew.

Remember, it's hard to scale your passion alone. You've no doubt heard of this African proverb: "To go fast, go alone; to go far, go together." And you and your crew have many miles to go to change the world.

Lew's Tips & Resources

Lew didn't say "do it fast." He said "do it right." He understood that to truly make a difference, you needed other people to join you on the journey. If you are on a big adventure, a quest with other like-minded changemakers, you will need a pace that can allow for maximum impact.

Maxim 1: Make a Difference

- **Establish corporate rhythm:** Establish a corporate rhythm that allows for strategic discussions to breathe and ensures alignment within the team.
- **Make the main thing the main thing:** Start all meetings with purpose and the flight plan.
- **Differentiate between tactical and strategic meetings:** Schedule regular strategic meetings (monthly, quarterly) to focus on the purpose, the bigger picture, and making meaningful decisions that drive the company forward. Focus weekly meetings on getting things done!

Maxim 2: Be Bold

- **Schedule the year:** Implement a structured approach to meetings, separating tactical discussions from strategic ones, to drive efficiency and productivity.
- **Be curious:** Avoid excessive approval seeking, and embrace curiosity and openness when facing disagreements or pushback.

Maxim 3: Do It Right

- **Use CPR:** Use the CPR (context, purpose, result) framework to bring clarity to meetings, ensuring that participants are purposefully matched with problem-solving.
- **Optimize energy and focus:** Proactively structure your schedule to optimize energy and focus, ensuring that individual meetings feed into larger group meetings and support the company's purpose and goals.

Books or Articles to Consider
- *Death by Meeting* by Patrick Lencioni
- *The 15 Commitments of Conscious Leadership* by Jim Dethmer, Diana Chapman, and Kaley Klemp

Scale Passion Resources
- "Running a Retreat Workshop": a guided approach to running a two-day strategic retreat
- Scale Passion meeting templates and workbooks: a comprehensive approach to running meetings

Find a comprehensive list of resources at ScalePassion.com/Resources.

Chapter 11

STOP! DO NOT PASS GO!

f you're reading this chapter, you have either read through the first two parts of the book and done the hard work of discovering your superpowers, unleashing your purpose and building a leadership team that can help you scale this purpose, *or* . . . you have not done the work and hoped instead to skip merrily ahead to the third stage of scaling your passion. I hate to be the one to tell you this—actually, I love to be the one telling you this—but you can't move on to stage 3 without doing the work of stages 1 and 2.

It can't be done. You can try it, but you'll fail because you will be attempting to lead from a place of inauthenticity. I know this because I have worked with many leaders who see purpose as a side of fries they want to get along with their strategic burger. Their business is stuck, and they're burning out and don't know how to get unstuck operationally, so they want to engage my team to help them build a strategic plan, hire and fire some people, put out infernos real and imagined that have smoldered too long, and help them become better, more efficient, more effective leaders.

I say yes to all those little burgers, but I add that if purpose isn't baked into them, they will be better served elsewhere. There are a lot of other consultants and businesses that can help you make more money, but we're in the business of helping you make a difference as well as more money.

And *difference* isn't a pill you can take. No, difference is a state of mind, a mindset, that must be earned by being bold enough to stand for something beyond your profit and loss statement. Making a difference requires you to tap into the energy that flows naturally and prodigiously from knowing your purpose and applying your superpower toward achieving it.

Are you bold enough to commit to doing this work? If you aren't, you can't have that company we profiled in the introduction. Who's going to follow you and step up and think like a change-the-world business owner if you haven't done the work yourself? Do you remember the great and chilling film adaptation of the play *Glengarry Glen Ross* in which the Alec Baldwin character tells the Jack Lemmon character that coffee was "only for closers"?

Well, stage 3 is only for closers.

In stage 2, we applied my dad's "do it right" principle to show how, once you have unleashed your purpose within yourself, you can begin building out a leadership team and strategy that can help you construct an organization to scale that purpose. After all, you can't scale your passion alone; you need to surround yourself with people who are smarter than you in their respective fields but share a capacity for strategic thinking and "laying track," as I like to say, for your company's future. You achieve this by deploying your purpose, as well as clarity, alignment, and pace, to create the foundation of what will become a very special and inspirational culture—a way of *doing it right*—for which your company will be known far and wide.

Everything I wrote in that introduction was true. That company wasn't a fantasy or an ideal; it was a real, ongoing concern that was, perhaps, a year or so away from becoming a self-managed company. "Whoa!" you say. "What's this about self-managed companies?"

Exactly!

That's what we're going to explore in stage 3!

Except you can't join us.

Unless, of course, you've done the work of putting yourself out there. Of closing on your purpose and putting in place a plan to bring a leadership team along with you.

Like Jordan Rubin did when he wrote about his illness in a book called *Patient Heal Thyself* and put himself on the cover as a six-foot-one-inch package of skin and bones in nothing but shorts to show how he discovered his purpose of making people well outside of pharmaceuticals and the allopathic medicine community.

When we met, he didn't know squat about marketing or packaging or distribution or strategic planning. But he knew one thing: it sucked to feel crappy all the time, and enough people agreed with him that he dedicated a part of his life to helping people feel healthier.

Like former professional football player Jeff Byers did when he decided that the public had been poorly served by the performance supplement industry for far too long and cofounded a science-based company to democratize high performance for the average athlete and even nonathlete. Jeff didn't know much about the science of supplements prior to founding Momentous, but he sure understood the mental, physical, and psychological health benefits of performing at the highest level. And he saw absolutely no reason why you had to be six-foot-four with three hundred pounds of muscle (his playing weight) to enjoy feeling this way.

Do you see where we're going with this? This is the kind of passion that needs to be scaled. It doesn't have to be through something you ingest. Yvon Chouinard felt passionate about preserving the ecosystems that nourished his heart, mind, and soul, even if that came to mean buying back the stuff he sold to people and making Earth his company's sole shareholder.

So, let me ask you again: Are you prepared to be the spark that lights the fire of purpose and passion in your organization? Once you go down this path, you will likely stay on it through thick and thin.

So, what was that personal purpose again?

I exist to _____

_____.

And, here's a great place to capture the work you put in from chapter 7 on your company's purpose:

We exist to _____

_____.

Only if you are ready, willing, and committed . . . turn the page.

RADIATE PURPOSE AND IMPACT

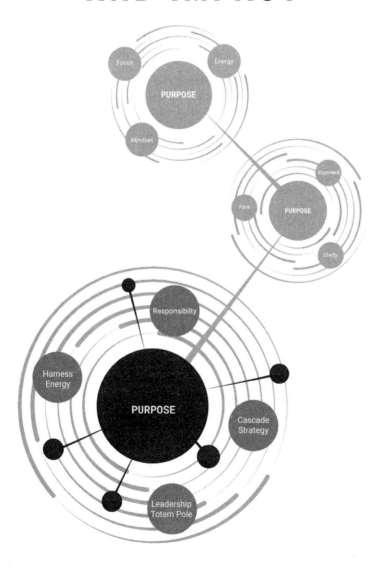

Chapter 12

Spark #1: Deepen the Leadership Totem Pole

'll never forget the day in 2016.

There I was, five years into my tenure as CEO of MegaFood, sitting in my office crunching some numbers, when into my office marched one of our top directors.

"Robert, I wondered whether I might make a presentation at next week's retreat?" he asked me.

He had a compelling idea that he was fired up about. He had written up a Blue Sheet proposal. (A Blue Sheet was the tool we used to train our directors how to write proposals.)

I gave the proposal a quick scan, and it seemed well thought out, so I told him I would work him into the agenda, and at the following week's strategic retreat, he made the two-hour trip to meet us there to present his idea for an hour. He was sky-high excited for the occasion, and frankly, so was I because I loved seeing the first instance of our directors truly running the business.

Remember, our goal was that our directors became fully responsible for running the day-to-day business with the responsibility on the executive leadership team to hire the right people and train them to do just that.

In a way, I often think of that day as a highlight in my career as a CEO, when I truly felt like the company had reached a tipping point. This director's example rapidly spread to other directors, as I used my platform as CEO to highlight his efforts and leadership at town halls and in my other communications.

Once you have harnessed your own purpose and positioned a leadership team to help you scale it through the company, you are ready to do the most important thing a change-the-world business owner can do: stop working *in* your business and begin working *on* it.

The leadership totem pole is a visual metaphor that illustrates why leaders can only radiate purpose and impact when they have strong shoulders to sit on. The higher up the totem pole you reside, the farther out you can see. There is no best place to be on the totem pole because everyone has a responsibility to focus on something important. For example, those on the bottom may see the least far ahead, but they are probably looking directly into the eyes of the customer; their place in the organization is vital to its success. The director-level folks in the middle are critical because they translate strategy and customer and market input up and down the pole. While VPs are plotting the course, directors are the ones agilely running the show. They ensure alignment up and down the totem pole.

The key function of the totem pole metaphor is to get you, the founder or CEO, as high above the day-to-day view as possible so you can inspire stakeholders with the company's purpose.

When I joined Garden of Life, founder Jordan Rubin was operating at the bottom of the totem pole. He was literally designing and selling the product. So, we built a totem pole beneath him. We hired product development experts and great R&D people and top sales and marketing minds.

We extended the new product release times to allow for greater inputs before investing resources in production.

And what happened? Jordan could think more clearly and look further ahead. He broadened his impact by writing a new book aimed at supporting his growing understanding of empowering human health. His book opened entirely new markets for his first company and helped him open a second company that sold another line of products to a different kind of customer. He was able to envision something completely new and touch millions more people he probably never would have touched if he had just stayed working *in* the business.

In my own company, ScalePassion, my purpose is to help business owners scale their purposes, and we are building a totem pole to help us realize this goal. When I started the company, I did everything myself. I did the personal purpose coaching we discussed in stage 1; I did the corporate purpose development and strategy coaching we covered in stage 2; and I did the exponential purpose development work we are now covering in stage 3. On the business side, I did all the business development. I even designed and created all the copy for the website. I was up to my eyeballs in the business.

Then, I began to build my own totem pole by bringing in some great people to lead these areas of the business. And, lo and behold, every one of these key areas is in the capable hands of others who are not only great at what they do but also share my passion for boldly making a difference in the world and treating people right.

As Dan Sullivan wrote in *Who Not How*, I put less focus on figuring out how I would run the business and more focus on who I could inspire to help me run and grow it. Aligned around the vision, we nailed our flight plan and began thinking in larger terms about exponential purpose. That's where this book comes in, as well as other initiatives we have planned, none of which could happen if I were still bringing in 100% of the business and doing all the coaching!

Why Did the Chicken Cross the Road?

Let me tell you a quick story about Matt O'Hayer. Matt was a serial entrepreneur who says he found success when he "stopped trying to get rich" and
found a business with a "deeper purpose." For Matt, that purpose became
running a profitable poultry business that recognized the needs of all stakeholders. This included the people who worked the farms that produced the
chickens, the chickens themselves, the land that supported the enterprise,
and the customers who wanted nutritious food. In 2007, he brought his vision
to life by buying 27 acres near Austin, Texas, and started raising chickens and
cows and selling eggs and butter. He named the enterprise Vital Farms.

Matt said that when they started Vital Farms, 90% of the eggs that were
being produced in the United States came from industrial farms where
chickens lived in cages too small to allow any movement. Anybody who
has read Eric Schlosser's *Fast Food Nation* knows all too well about such
practices. In the beginning, Matt built his business from the ground up,
spending the first few years learning the ins and outs of organic farming,
crop rotation, and how to sell premium poultry products to customers.
Eventually, Vital Farms began to gain traction as customers were willing
to pay more for better-tasting, humanely grown eggs.

As the business grew, Matt stepped up his role as a leader in the
pasture-raised or free-range chicken movement. He left the day-to-day
management to his growing team and fixed his gaze on providing leadership to an industry that needed reform. His focus shifted from his product
to how his business was helping hundreds of farmers, millions of customers, and billions of chickens live better lives. And as he does this, Vital
Farms is growing into a business that Matt told CNBC should bring in
more than $1 billion in annual net revenue by 2027.

And that, my friend, adds up to a lot fewer chickens living in cages.

Do you think Matt could have built a company with such impact if he
were still tending to the chickens on a daily basis?

It's All About Training

Business tycoon Richard Branson said, "Train people well enough so they can leave, treat them well enough so they don't want to." Large companies can rely on standard operating procedures to guide their directors. But fast-growing, entrepreneurial companies need to train their directors to develop greater capacity as planners and build alignment within the business. How do you train your directors well enough to allow yourself and your executive team to entrust the day-to-day entirely to their capable hands? In each of the organizations I've been a part of, we tackled this challenge through something I call Flight School.

Flight School is a homegrown training program that helps plant the leadership totem deep into the culture of the organization. Flight School helps change-the-world leaders and their teams grow their personal leadership and their capacity to lead others. Using many of the principles (and the books) referenced in this book, we begin with leadership first principles. These include what traits, qualities, skills, and behaviors a leader should have. Obviously, this begins with personal purpose and self-leadership, which includes taking 100% responsibility, cultivating a growth mindset, and following many of the principles discussed in the first part of this book. Then we teach scaling purpose and leading others with an emphasis on leading with integrity, building high-trust teams, and reducing drama in the workplace, since drama does more than anything else to undermine performance over the long run.

We fine-tuned Flight School to the degree that it includes not only leading yourself and leading others but also leading other leaders, as different skills and knowledge bases are required to manage directors compared to hourly workers, just to offer one example.

One of the ways we operationalize the teaching and coaching from Flight School is to hold our quarterly all-hands leadership meeting—which includes select managers, directors, and executive leaders—right before our quarterly executive retreat. We use the leadership quarterly—training and input gathering—meeting to give the directors a forum for sharing their ideas about their respective areas and what they're seeing in the marketplace, including pain points and trends. It's critical that your directors, despite being in the middle of the leadership totem pole, see their contribution to strategy (see chapter 8).

Here are some simple questions and actions that might help you to start your own Flight School:

1. What qualities do we want in our leaders?
2. Who are the leaders in our organization that need to be trained? (Now designate them to small groups of no more than four to five.)
3. What authors, books, and approaches do we think will help us develop these qualities in our leaders? (Now, prioritize the list.)
4. Which executive leader has real passion around a subject? (Now designate them to teach the lesson.)

Last, schedule six one-hour Flight School sessions every other week each quarter to teach these leaders in 20- to 30-minute lessons on the topic. Leave the remaining time for group discussion, challenges, and application.

Sometimes You Win, Sometimes You Learn

As a leader, you need to fail as quickly and early on as possible so that you can learn from your failures and apply that learning. The same thing is true for your leadership team. You have to make it safe and constructive to fail. In my companies, I couldn't wait for our first project, initiative, or OKR to go sideways because every time we did a postmortem of the failure, we made ourselves that much better.

But learning how to learn takes intentional, concerted effort, which is why I make it a point to conduct postmortems on a project or process or event or even a conversation that went wrong—and even sometimes when things go very right. It's about evaluating something in the past to learn from it. A useful postmortem includes fully evaluating the situation from beginning to end, identifying and capturing key learnings and lessons, and most importantly, identifying the tangible steps you and your team will take to ensure that these learnings are redirected or reflected in new projects and tasks going forward. (Note: leaders who are *in* the business can never seem to find the time to lead a postmortem.) Remember, it's not enough just to learn; you also want to improve your processes and make your business stronger for the long run.

Every postmortem needs a moderator who doesn't necessarily have to be the leader. I generally like to book an hour for a postmortem. A postmortem should have the following general flow:

1. Set a positive tone and explain the purpose of the meeting— explain that the goal is to learn, not to place blame (5 minutes).
2. Recap the project (2 to 3 minutes).
3. Recap the outcome of the project (3 minutes).
4. Fill out the key postmortem questions together in the "Pink Sheet Postmortem" (see Scale Passion resources) (40 minutes).
5. Wrap up by clearly capturing key learnings and establishing new team norms (10 minutes).

By asking what methods or processes went well and what didn't, you are likely to find that many projects were not total failures but fell below expectations for some or all of those involved. Once you get the ball rolling and the conversation starts flowing, enlist the team in using what they've learned to generate ideas to use in the future.

Topgrading

Topgrading earned a bad reputation, and deservedly so, through its use by those like GE's Jack Welch, who used the method to summarily fire the *bottom* 10% of his workforce—however the bottom was defined. But when done in a more humane fashion, topgrading your organization is imperative.

Every person on your team should possess the knowledge, skills, and experience required for their role. If they don't, they must either be trained up or repositioned within or outside the company. This process demands decisiveness and a commitment to the long-term vision. Cultural fit should never be compromised, even if it means parting ways with a valuable team member. A cohesive culture ensures that everyone is aligned with the company's core values and objectives.

My experience with topgrading has been to evaluate people according to three different ratings. The first involves leadership potential, or promotability, which is color-coded as follows:

- *Green* employees are those who are promotable more than one level.
- *Yellow* employees are those who are promotable one level.
- *Red* employees are those who are not promotable.

The second metric we use involves "fit to role," or all the skills, knowledge, and experience a person needs to fit perfectly into their role. This metric involves an ABC rating as follows:

- An *A* employee is a perfect fit for their position at the time of evaluation.
- A *B* employee is a good fit for their position and can improve with additional time or training.

- A *C* employee does not fit their role within the culture and should either be moved somewhere else in the company or outside the company.

The third metric, which I won't elucidate here, is performance, which was usually independent of promotability or fit to role, although C employees were often also poor performers for obvious reasons.

One fallacy in thinking about topgrading is wanting your workforce to consist mostly of A-Green employees. A more sustainable mix would put the percentage of A-Red and B-Red employees at 50% to 60% of your team. After all, these are team members who are good at what they do and aren't necessarily looking for advancement. They are more likely to be happy, thus reducing drama and improving turnover. Too many Greens in a specific department sets yourself up for potential drama because they are energized to advance in the company and demand special treatment. Two or three Greens and Yellows at the director level per department is more than enough.

Maintain this balance as you go up the corporate ladder. A-Green, B-Green, A-Yellow, and B-Yellow employees are your future leaders and have the greatest capacity to grow and help you grow your business. Support these burgeoning leaders in a proactive way.

At MegaFood, Bethany Davis worked in our regulatory department and showed great leadership potential while being only a good rather than great fit to role. We sat down and discussed what she wanted in life, and her passion for the planet came shining through. She became a key player in our regenerative initiatives as our director of impact under Sara Newmark, our VP of impact, and while at MegaFood, she became passionate about conscious leadership. She became certified in the 15 Commitments of Conscious Leadership and today views herself as a champion of integrity and "doing things right."

Moving Bethany into a place where she could really express her purpose not only fired her up but also made her more impactful as a teammate. Bethany's example convinced me to make "strength of purpose" a key criterion for promotability in any organization I lead. But the point of topgrading isn't simply to classify your team and move the underperformers out; the point is to train and retain your best people, the future leaders who will take their place in your leadership totem pole. I make it a point to mentor my Greens by giving them special projects, bringing them to important meetings or conferences, or simply taking them to lunch to learn more about them and their goals.

In the organizations I have led, I scheduled topgrading in the lead-up to my executive team's October retreat, and it would drive hiring decisions for the coming year. Again, unless you and your leadership team have trained and empowered the directors to run the business, you and your leadership team likely will not have the capacity or time to do a proper job of topgrading across the organization. I gave my vice presidents lots of responsibility within their own units for setting goals, managing budgets, and producing results, but I did reserve for myself veto power on all hires at and above the director level because, as the CEO, I was ultimately responsible for the culture.

Empowerment Is the Key

As a business owner, you will greatly benefit by empowering your team to the broadest possible extent. This is far, far harder than it sounds. I know too many leaders who are afraid to share important figures, such as sales, profits, and other important numbers, and who don't trust their leadership team to set their own goals and challenge their employees.

My experience tells me the opposite: those in whom you entrust more power will habitually overreach rather than underreach, which carries its own set of challenges on which you, as the business owner, will have to work with them. Extending trust is way more fun and offers more opportunity for learning—for both you and your direct report.

Let's say you have hired some new people—people with serious marketing, sales, and operations chops—who you looked to for additional leadership as you grew from your handful to several dozen people. The idea was to empower your vice presidents and directors to run the business so you could get out in front of it by more than a few days or hours. And you did empower them. You spent time helping them understand your values and mission so they could help you take your company to the next level. Those retreats that are happening every 90 days or so are serving their purpose. You have an aligned, clear flight plan that your entire company, especially your leaders, can use to accelerate the business. The problem—admit it—is that your empowerment only extends through periods when things are going well. It tends to fall apart when, halfway through the month, something goes sideways or not according to plan and fear sets in.

A couple of missed sales or revenue goals and all that careful work you put in to empower your new leadership vanishes in an all-hands-on-deck call to get those numbers up today!

Sound familiar? I know you're scared of not hitting your revenue or monthly sales goal because those 50 salaries and all that overhead aren't going to pay for themselves. But you have to remember that a goal is not a strategy. Meeting a sales goal won't get you safely through the high-growth phase because this phase requires that you become more strategic and long-term in your thinking. You have to get past this idea that navigating the fast-growth phase means meeting one monthly revenue or sales goal after another.

Can you get past this? I think you have to.

When you pull every member of your team off whatever they're doing halfway through each month to meet your goal, you are effectively hitting a restart on your growth plan every month. I've seen this done before, and it won't work. You will lose people. You will lose market share. You will lose your passion for what got you there.

The solution is to return to your flight plan, the one you noodled with on your own, then nailed with your team, that defined who you are, who your customer and market are, what you stand for in the deepest possible way, and what is most important to do right now. Up to a point, this may have meant trying to be a lot of things to a lot of people, but now this has changed. You did your research and planning and realized you have reached a point where you need to focus on generating the right kind of sales to the right kind of customer.

So be brave and do it. You've hired good people and trained them and given them the strategy or playbook they need to make good decisions without you. That's how you scale, right? Scaling is a process. It may take many months or, more likely, several years with all the usual ups and downs to begin working. It rarely, and probably never, works by whip-sawing back and forth every month as budgeting forecasts are met or not.

Let me leave you with this suggestion. You got to where you are today by trusting your gut and inspiring others with your vision. I urge you to see your decision to scale your business by empowering others to run the day-to-day as a smart one and a good gut call on your part. Follow your head and your gut and focus on easing off the control switch and building that totem pole another foot higher.

Lew's Tips & Resources

When my dad realized he may have only a few years left, he spent that time pouring his knowledge and values into me. This took courage and vision. Let me encourage you to have that same courage and vision and empower your team. Train them up so that they can run your company, then watch how this frees you up to expand your purpose and impact!

Maxim 1: Make a Difference

- **Lead with purpose:** As the founder or CEO, focus on inspiring stakeholders with the company's purpose. Elevate yourself above the day-to-day view to envision a broader impact.
- **Empower others:** Build a leadership totem pole by hiring great leaders and delegating responsibilities. Trust your team to run the business while you focus on strategic direction.

Maxim 2: Be Bold

- **Invest in training:** Establish a training program like Flight School to develop leadership skills within your organization. Prioritize self-leadership, integrity, and building high-trust teams.
- **Encourage learning from failure:** Create a culture where it's safe to fail and learn. Conduct postmortems on projects or processes to identify key learnings and improve future initiatives.

Maxim 3: Do It Right

- **Implement topgrading:** Evaluate team members based on leadership potential, fit to role, and performance. Train and retain top performers while aligning them with the company's core values and objectives.

- **Empowerment and strategy:** Extend trust to your team and empower them to make decisions without micromanagement. Focus on long-term strategic planning rather than short-term revenue goals.

Books or Articles to Consider
- *Fast Food Nation* by Eric Schlosser
- *Topgrading* by Bradford Smart
- *Who* by Geoff Smart and Randy Street

Scale Passion Resources
- Flight School: a guided leadership training program for companies looking to harness purpose
- "Pink Sheet Postmortem": a guide for hosting a project postmortem

Find a comprehensive list of resources at ScalePassion.com/Resources.

Chapter 13

Spark #2: Responsibility over Accountability

By the time I walked into the Hilton in downtown Manchester, New Hampshire, on a chilly day in 2017, the snowball fight had already begun. They were flying everywhere: across the auditorium where the tables and chairs were set in front of the stage and across the reception area adjacent to the meeting room where the warming trays were being readied for the feast that would follow the company-wide meeting. I was the CEO of the company, but I didn't make it halfway to the stage without getting pelted by more than a few well-aimed fleece snowballs.

Welcome to the MegaFood town hall. (You know, the one I mentioned way back in chapter 3.) This wasn't just any company-wide meeting; it was the one in which we would formally announce the biggest pivot in the company's history. I wanted to position this pivot in the best possible light and came up with the idea of an expedition up Mount Everest. But rather than confine the analogy to my spoken remarks, we decided to turn the entire meeting into a metaphor.

There was even an oxygen bar next to the food.

I mean, you need plenty of oxygen if you're going to be climbing Mount Everest!

With my vision and Ashley Larochelle's leadership—Ashley was the vision activator in chapter 3—the event was a resounding success, which is to say that it was fun and people who had never had a strategic pivot explained to them in their entire careers understood what we were going to do. And the pivot was also successful, which is to say we created a direct-to-consumer channel to complement our retail strategy and better serve our customers. And we moved strongly toward transitioning our internal team from being people we could count on to do what we told them to do to people we could trust to take responsibility for their work and, more importantly, the business.

I relate this story to you to furnish a counterintuitive point about the journey all companies take as they move from their infancy through adolescence and into the prime of their lives, to borrow the corporate lifespan analogy created by the great professor Ichak Adizes. Businesspeople read a lot about the importance of accountability as a core value, but my experience has shown me that accountability is only the second stage of development a maturing company undergoes.

As we discussed in chapter 6, the first stage is autocracy, the stage at which a business owner runs the show and there is no leadership team, whatsoever, with any real power. This is very common with founders. Gradually, the autocrat must empower others at least a little bit to survive, so he or she makes them "accountable" by being required or expected to justify any decision they make, with the business owner retaining full veto power over every decision. As the organization grows, however, and the business owner cannot possibly stay on top of all the people and processes that have sprung up, a measure of "autonomy" is extended to the leadership team and their departments. The leadership team together set the objectives—the *what*—but everyone else is given latitude to meet those expectations with more or less control over *how* they do it.

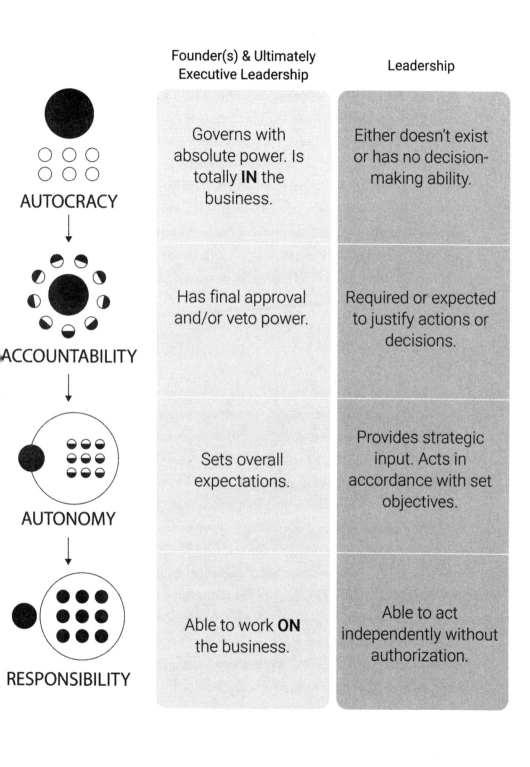

	Founder(s) & Ultimately Executive Leadership	Leadership
AUTOCRACY	Governs with absolute power. Is totally **IN** the business.	Either doesn't exist or has no decision-making ability.
ACCOUNTABILITY	Has final approval and/or veto power.	Required or expected to justify actions or decisions.
AUTONOMY	Sets overall expectations.	Provides strategic input. Acts in accordance with set objectives.
RESPONSIBILITY	Able to work **ON** the business.	Able to act independently without authorization.

In the first two phases especially, and sometimes even in the third phase, the business owner is still working *in* the day-to-day aspects of the business, albeit even further removed from the customer than the rest of the team. It is only when the business enters the fourth stage that the larger team enjoys true "responsibility," which means they work independently as self-managed teams without having the founder or CEO authorizing most decisions.

Most companies never reach this fourth stage for a variety of reasons. In this chapter, we'll look at the three variables—trust, shared purpose, and empowerment—that powerfully influence a business owner's relationship with their teams and whose presence, or absence, will determine whether an organization can become self-managed.

Trust Is a Two-Way Street

I can't ask you to be trustworthy if I'm not willing to extend some trust to you. The Mount Everest event and our subsequent pivot represented a big win for the company, but it would have been much harder, if not impossible, to carry out without extending trust to my team. With empowerment comes responsibility. Your transformational goal in raising a change-the-world culture is to shift the responsibility for creating impact from yourself to your internal team and, eventually, your external stakeholders. But let's stick with the internal team first.

I'm a big believer in professional development not only, or even mainly, for improving hard skills but also for becoming more independent, autonomous, and, ultimately, responsible for everything you do. There are many other tools that help in this regard. As I wrote in the previous chapter, one of those tools is a fully baked leadership development program, such as Flight School, in addition to professional and skills-based development. But there are other tools too.

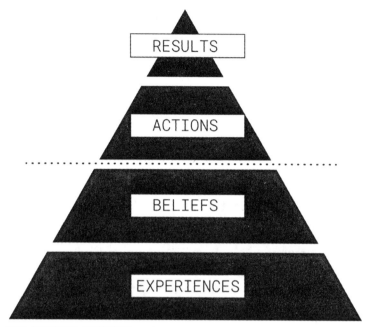

THE RESULTS PYRAMID®

Look at the figure above, which is my twist on a "results pyramid" coined by authors Roger Connors and Tom Smith in *Change in Culture, Change the Game*. This construct is based on the belief that to scale a business and its purpose, you have to establish a foundation in *experiences* for your team that will create *beliefs* in the company's purpose—in Mega-Food's case, this meant helping a world in nutritional crisis—which will, in turn, generate *actions* that will eventuate in the final *result*. The result, by the way, isn't just a revenue or profit figure; these are metrics that show us how well we are achieving our purpose of changing the world. But the two goals—profit and impact—go hand in hand in mutual advancement or regression. In our case, it was continual advancement.

As the leader, I was constantly on the lookout for ways to tap into my team's superpowers in the hope of connecting them to our larger purpose. Ashley was one shining example, but there were many others. As I was making calls with a sales rep to assess our product placement, pricing, and customer attitudes, I noticed that the rep had a remarkable awareness of what our competition was doing: "Man, I can't believe that [so and so company] is getting away with that pricing," he'd observe. Or, "Did you notice that new product [so and so] just came out with? We should be there too!"

He told me he loved getting to know the competition inside and out, so I ventured a question.

"How would you like to be our competition czar?" I asked.

"Oh, man. I'd love to do that," he said, his face lighting up. "So, what is a competition czar?"

"Okay," I said. "So, two weeks before my leadership team's quarterly retreat, I want a list as detailed or simple as you want covering our competition. I'll clear this with your director and vice president."

And I had it two weeks before my retreat so that we could use it as input for our planning. He took full responsibility for reaching out to all the other sales reps in the field via phone or email and collected tons of data. He effectively became a lateral leader among his peers and, best of all, felt his energy go up as his competitive fire was kindled by the opportunity to do something he was passionate about. I never missed another new product or initiative from a competitor.

Toward Self-Managing Teams

When you use experiences like these to make responsibility a core value—one of our early core values was actually "thinking like an owner"—you build a framework in which self-managing teams can begin to flourish. The advantages of self-managing teams are twofold: first, in the long term, it allows your leadership to work *on* the business rather than *in* it; second, it allows you to make decisions closer to where your customer lives, which is out at the edge of where traditional corporate power is exercised.

At MegaFood, we used a software program called GlassFrog, which describes its use as agile team management, another way of saying self-managing teams. (You could use many different types of project management software to set up and operate this kind of system.) This particular program lets you create a business within a business that comprises circles within circles of strategic work groups. All circles exist within the largest circle of the executive leadership team, which supports the organization's overall mission and purpose. All circles are cross-functional. The rationale for this cross-functionality is that most important strategic matters involve people from different areas who hold a piece of the puzzle in their hands. Each circle has to have a purpose, as well as strategies and objectives and specific roles assigned to every member.

In addition, each circle leader gets to recruit whomever they think will best contribute to the circle, including those senior to them. To give you an example of how this can work, during our pivot to omnichannel at Mega-Food, we created a circle called "Remarkable Omnichannel Experience." The leader was a senior member of the executive team who recruited me to the circle for my visionary skills. This didn't mean I was the leader of the circle or responsible for the successful execution of its objectives. That fell to the leader/circle leader who recruited each circle member to fill a specific role.

Within this circle, it became clear that we needed a special focus on e-commerce, so one member of the team who had more of this kind of experience than anyone else created a subcircle in which she was the leader, reporting out to the leader of the omnichannel circle. But just think about this for a moment: Here you had someone three levels junior to me leading a group I was in. Making the calls and doing a great job of it. Yes, decisions of a certain magnitude needed to be cleared by higher circles, including the executive leadership circle that I led, but this method created greater efficiencies than we could possibly have enjoyed using a traditional, top-heavy, highly centralized leadership model. Not to mention the empowered leaders (and the amazing energy that comes with them) that it produced.

Beat That Bass Drum

If you had to describe the typical rhythm of your company, would it be more like a jazz session or a marching band number? As a longtime drummer, I've played in both kinds of bands—and even played in a rock band—and loved all of them, but I also know that jazz and marches are completely different animals, with different expectations for how you work together.

Over the last 30-something years of working with business owners and their teams, I feel confident saying that much of the time younger founders think of their business more like playing jazz. In jazz, you sit down with a group of talented players and let the music take you where it wants to go. Someone might throw a riff out there, and the other members of the band might grab that riff, or they might keep going with their own thing. Another time, a different player might throw out a riff, and the whole team might take a left turn and flow with that. This means you can start to develop a different tempo and a different rhythm and a completely different melody—sometimes on the fly. Young companies might feel comfortable improvising like this and placing lots of little bets to see what sticks and doesn't stick.

Once a company has figured out their product, their pricing model, their brand strategy, and the perfect sales channels they should be in, it's time to put away the beret, shave the soul patch, and reach into the armoire for something with a gator, wildcat, eagle, bulldog, or Spartan on the front. It's time to begin thinking like a marching band!

The truth is that jazz is an acquired taste that seems strange to many people, particularly those who have spent a fair amount of time in larger corporations. They're used to marching to the beat of the bass drum that sets the tempo for everyone to follow. Marching bands are a blast because the camaraderie is terrific and everybody knows their contribution to the music. It might be three minutes or four minutes or 10 minutes, and then you change to a new song—but every musician knows what's happening and can play and step in sync.

Let's dig down a little more. The marching band is driven by the bass drum, which sets the tempo for everyone to follow and keeps them on schedule with regular meetings each week, month, and quarter. Unlike jazz, which lives in the minds of the players, the marching band music is written in the score (read: flight plan), which furnishes the score everybody follows, more or less, to the note.

The score makes everybody feel comfortable because it tells them where to go.

There is still some room for solos and riffs, but these are written into the music (read: the flight plan). For example, the young jazz start-up might launch a new "minimal viable product" riff every quarter just to see what concepts gain traction among its customers, then adjust based on the results. With an MVP, you try something small and contained with a clear objective, and you assign a very specific team who have a very specific set of objectives and a very specific budget that keeps it contained.

As the leader, you're beating the bass drum. There are many different rhythms you might play, but I prefer to communicate in an intentional way by dividing meetings into strategic or tactical ones, and by having the departmental meetings feed the more centralized executive leadership meetings. For instance, each individual reports to a manager, who reports to a director, who reports to a vice president, who reports to the leader. These meetings can either happen with a fair degree of randomness, which is usually the case, or they can be organized as a pipeline of actionable information sharing, which is far less often what happens but has the advantage of giving otherwise disparate meetings a common purpose. I call the second method smart calendaring because every meeting lives within a meaningful context with every other meeting.

I have also made a practice of doing departmental roundtables every six to eight weeks in which I sit down with 10 to 20 people in an area of the company to talk about the company. I never push an agenda and, to the contrary, put the entire onus of conversation on the employees, who are free to ask me anything they want. I noticed a shift in the kinds of topics the teams asked me. For example, in the earlier roundtables, people tended to focus on issues of security, such as benefits, layoffs, and the like. As time went on, they asked about topics such as innovation, new product ideas, and various efficiencies, which they had noted in the course of their work.

The roundtables gave me not only some good ideas and a direct insight into conversations within the company but also the opportunity to take every question and place it in the context of our purpose, mission, core values, and OKRs. The roundtables informed my senior leadership meetings and our board meetings. I always made sure our board had a place in our town hall meetings because it allowed board members to experience our culture firsthand.

On the Monday after a big road trip and client visit week, I made a voice memo that I sent to the entire company, offering an inspirational story from my travels that exemplified our purpose in action. It may have focused on a core value being lived out with a sales rep going the extra mile for a customer or an illustration of corporate shared value manifesting itself in the success of one of our farming partnerships.

Always banging the drum.

I Got Your Number(s)

You can't ask your employees to think like owners and support your strategy if you don't help them understand the financial side of your organization. I am a fan of a classic book by Jack Stack called *The Great Game of Business*. It's been around for decades but still inspires me. Stack is called the father of open book transparency for the way he shared the financials of his machine-making company with his employees. He'd get them all in an auditorium and, using an overhead projector, would go through the P&L figures for every department.

He didn't just share the numbers; he spent money training his employees to understand the financial statements and balance sheets so that they could understand the business better. And he then spent money to train them so they could understand the numbers. If you want to ask people to understand the little measures they can take to save money or make more money, you need to teach them how a lot of little decisions impact the bottom line. Sharing the financials doesn't mean you have to share everything—you may not want to share your salary, for instance—but it makes your employees feel more responsible for the company.

I have found that finance-savvy employees also appreciate what such training does for their ability to manage their personal finances, which involves much of the same kind of balancing act required in business.

When you think about sharing numbers, don't just think about operational costs or P&L. Find ways to connect financial literacy to your purpose. Many firms publish impact statements that show exactly how much of a difference they make in the world through their purpose. At Patagonia, for example, they keep a running tab of the dollars directed toward nonprofit work through the company's 1% for the Planet initiative. At MegaFood, we tracked in real time on a big old scoreboard the number of lives our products improved every day.

Give Your Culture a Name

I began banging the drum the day I arrived at MegaFood when I put up whiteboards in key meeting areas and posed questions to our team: "What do we stand for?" "How do we behave toward one another?" and "What qualities do we look for in our teammates?" Then, I collected the answers to see what our team thought our current culture consisted of. My goal wasn't simply to learn what they thought but also to enlist them as agents in the changes we were going to be implementing in the company.

Yet another goal was to use this feedback to put a name on the company's culture, one that would not settle for describing what *had been* but rather would prime the pump for future change. And the nature of that change would be pushing for less autocracy and more responsibility from everyone in the company. When you're trying to change your culture, it helps to come up with a name for it that balances the present culture and the aspirational culture, allowing your team to see themselves as players in its construction and its evolution.

At MegaFood, we called it Zing Mojo, which we described as "the state of controlled craziness that comes when a group of people are in a hurry to deliver their mission of improving lives." It captured our ethos of responsible urgency and established the values that would guide how we worked together. The "way" consists of several key attributes: brave, trustworthy, grateful, and fun. These attributes also established the ground rules for how we work with our various stakeholders so that they know what to expect from us. This culture wasn't being developed randomly but rather as a necessary framework for becoming an exponential organization. It enabled us to identify new leaders as we grew, set expectations for various levels of leadership, and tap into some incredible energy from within the ranks.

Here are three examples of what I mean:

1. The operator of one of our refractance window dryers in our man-
    ufacturing area was inspired by seeing the way a dryer transforms
    beautiful whole foods into nutrient-packed powders. He wanted
    to tell the important story of what he did every day, so he started
    taking his camera to work and photographing cranberries and
    other foods and then posted them online, proving that storytell-
    ing can come from anywhere in our company.

2. A member of our strategic business group team felt our industry's
    biggest event, Expo West, offered a not-to-be-missed opportunity
    to reach out to our natural retail customers who were fighting for
    their survival in the age of Amazon Prime. The employee orga-
    nized a breakfast with a group of family-owned retail customers
    and me. We talked about the incredible pace of change, the chal-
    lenges facing our industry, and how retailers can compete with
    e-commerce. The breakfast also served to reassure our retail cus-
    tomers that we hadn't forgotten about them—an important mes-
    sage given the need for brands like MegaFood to pivot to a more
    consumer-facing position.

3. Our brand team recruited a group of consumers to do something
    we'd never tried: codevelop a new line of products—gummy sup-
    plements. How did we know they wanted gummies? We knew
    because they told us, and our team was listening. Our consumer
    MegaFoodies were with us from product development through
    testing, and they were on hand to receive our industry award for
    the best new supplement delivery format.

These may not seem like earth-shattering acts of initiative, but I've
always been inspired by this stuff because these actions start to express a
level of not only accountability and autonomy but also the responsibility
with which every true leader ought to strive to imbue his team.

Where on the journey from autocracy to responsibility is your organization's culture? And more to the aim of this book, what can you do right now to help your employees better connect the dots from your purpose to their day-to-day functions so that they feel inspired by your purpose so much that they feel responsible for its realization?

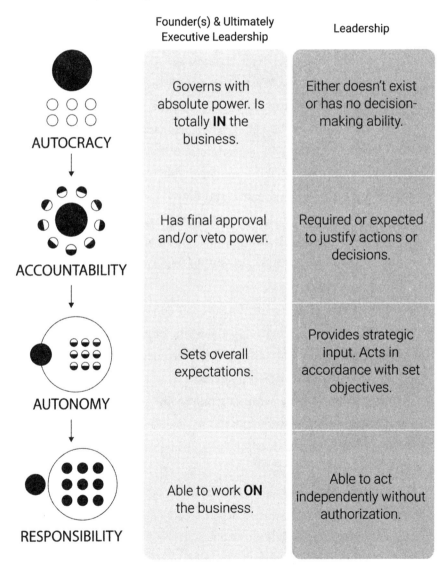

	Founder(s) & Ultimately Executive Leadership	Leadership
AUTOCRACY	Governs with absolute power. Is totally **IN** the business.	Either doesn't exist or has no decision-making ability.
ACCOUNTABILITY	Has final approval and/or veto power.	Required or expected to justify actions or decisions.
AUTONOMY	Sets overall expectations.	Provides strategic input. Acts in accordance with set objectives.
RESPONSIBILITY	Able to work **ON** the business.	Able to act independently without authorization.

Lew's Tips & Resources

Lew was the ultimate owner of everything in his life: not only his work but also the well-being of his family and community. He always took 100% responsibility for his actions and stood behind his decisions—even and *especially* when they were bold. Not many middle-aged men of his generation went back to school and started all over!

Maxim 1: Make a Difference

- **Extend trust:** Trust is a cornerstone of building a culture of responsibility. Business owners must be willing to extend trust to their teams, empowering them to take ownership of their work and contribute meaningfully to the company's goals.
- **Foster responsibility:** Provide employees with the autonomy to make decisions and execute tasks in alignment with the company's objectives. Empowering individuals to work independently fosters a sense of responsibility and accountability.
- **Encourage professional development:** Invest in employees' professional development to not only enhance their hard skills but also cultivate independence, autonomy, and a sense of responsibility for their work and the business as a whole.

Maxim 2: Be Bold

- **Embrace creativity:** Encourage creativity and innovation in problem-solving and decision-making. The chapter highlights creative approaches, such as using metaphors like the Mount Everest expedition to convey strategic pivots, as effective tools for engaging and inspiring teams.
- **Cultivate self-managing teams:** Foster self-managing teams by

providing tools and frameworks like GlassFrog for agile team management. Empower employees to take on leadership roles within their teams and make decisions closer to where the customer lives, promoting efficiency and empowerment.

- **Establish clear communication rhythms:** Create intentional communication rhythms within the organization, resembling a marching band's tempo. Regular meetings at strategic, tactical, and departmental levels facilitate alignment, collaboration, and accountability across the organization.

Maxim 3: Do It Right

- **Promote financial literacy:** Share financial information transparently with employees and invest in their financial literacy to help them understand how their actions impact the company's bottom line. This fosters a sense of responsibility and ownership among employees.
- **Name and define company culture:** Give the company's culture a distinct name and define its values to guide employee behavior and decision-making. Establishing a clear cultural identity, such as Zing Mojo, helps align employees with the company's purpose and goals.
- **Recognize and reward initiative:** Acknowledge and reward employees who demonstrate initiative and take ownership of their work. Highlighting examples of employee-driven initiatives, such as product development or customer outreach, reinforces a culture of responsibility and encourages others to follow suit.

Books or Articles to Consider

- *Change the Culture, Change the Game* by Roger Connors and Tom Smith

Tools to Consider
- GlassFrog: an approach to organizing self-managed teams (glassfrog.com)

Scale Passion Resources
- Flight School: a guided leadership training program for companies looking to harness purpose

Find a comprehensive list of resources at ScalePassion.com/Resources.

Chapter 14

Spark #3: Cascade Impact

When you're at the top of the totem pole of a responsible company and commanding a long view of the world, your marketplace, and your company, you are right where you should be to scale your impact. Freed from the tactical minutiae of working *in* the business, you can focus your sights *on* the business and, more importantly, on expanding your purpose and impact. And let me tell you, you'll enjoy an entirely new view from the top of the totem pole.

For starters, the further out you see, the more you will realize that the things you thought you understood about your company, customer, marketplace, product, priorities, and the whole world were shortsighted. You will see your marketplace not as a tooth-and-nail fight for shelf space and endcaps but as a space for understanding your customer's changing needs and identifying resources for satisfying those needs. You'll discover that your customer cares about things you never knew they did and shopped in ways you hadn't been able to anticipate when your nose was to the grindstone.

Over the past few years, one of the oft-cited cautionary phrases in explorations of leadership and strategy has been that "you don't know what you don't know." One of the many useful implications of this protean phrase is that your job as a business owner is to learn how to know what you don't know, which comes in handy when trying to anticipate change rather than merely react to it. The best place to do this is from the top of the totem pole.

When I was leading MegaFood, I attended an Abundance360 conference featuring Astro Teller, the former director of Google X, entrepreneur, and author. Teller spoke persuasively about the exponential pace of change made possible by technology and advocated for leaders to think about innovation and failure in a different light—one that celebrated failure as the necessary precursor of creative thinking. He often used the term *moonshot* to describe the kind of bold and creative thinking needed to harness technology to improve human health and quality of living. (I think of a moonshot in much the same terms as a BHAG.)

We launched our own moonshot of curing nutritional poverty even before I heard Teller speak, but we doubled down on this purpose by creating MegaFood Blue, based on Google X, and hired and funded Dr. Andrew Brandeis as our entrepreneur in residence. Andrew's job was to look at where the supplement industry and health and wellness in general were heading. He found that the technology-enabled customization of health and wellness was the answer, and while my tenure at the company ended before we could move meaningfully in that direction, Andrew made this insight the basis for his successful company, OK Capsule, which you read about earlier in this book.

Few companies hit the impact ground running, but once impact takes hold, you are off to the races. This chapter will take you through the exhilarating steps of putting the pieces and process in place that will enable you to cascade your purpose. This includes identifying an impact guru from within your company or hiring one to help weave purpose into the fabric of your business. This chapter also illustrates how much more powerful your marketing can be as your business, brand, and marketing strategy align ever closer, closing the gap between your product and purpose.

Find Your Impact Guru

Building your company on a strong foundation of purpose as well as profitability makes good business sense. As your company grows, the challenge comes in maintaining the passion that got you into the business in the first place. Even if you're the most committed founder, you know that at some point you'll need more help running the company.

You will hire an operations leader to make the trains run on time, a sales and marketing leader to reach your customers, a finance guru to make sure the numbers work in your favor, and eventually a leader to help you focus on the people and build the right kind of culture to deliver on the company's mission.

But what about impact? Where does that fit in the list of priorities? How do you hire to ensure that impact constantly cascades through your people and into everything you do? On the one hand, the whole point of this book is to argue that nothing can replace a totally engaged business owner as the company's impact champion. But eventually, you're going to have to create greater capacity for, and focus on, that piece of the pie just as surely as you would if sales or marketing were outside your zone of genius.

Before we get into titles, what you want to look for is a full-time person who can ensure that everything you do in your company reflects your purpose. The way you make and package things. The way you engage with retailers and customers. The people you partner with in your supply chain and as investors. If this sounds like a big job, that's because it is. Far too big for a founder or CEO who has to look at the whole picture. You might start out hiring a fractional chief impact officer to inventory and develop some ideas for your impact programs. I would recommend a director of impact, but regardless of the title or rank of your impact champion, they should have a seat on your leadership team.

If a reasonable budget for a chief impact officer (CIO) or director-level impact champion isn't in the cards, you can look at hiring an impact-minded graduate of one of the growing number of business school programs offering experiences or even degree programs that include strong sustainability or social-impact components.

In the best of all worlds, however, you'd find someone with the practical experience and leadership skills to fit that CIO position. Ideally, this contributor would be well connected to influencers, investors, and people in your industry who have a passion for impact that aligns with your company. It may be a former CEO who wants to focus on impact. Or it could be someone with a marketing background. We've known cases where retailers or buyers fit the bill as CIOs because they know how to think through a business plan that brings in partnerships with suppliers, manufacturers, and so on.

By sitting on your leadership team, the CIO will be well placed to cast a wide net over your company's impact programs. Think in terms of stakeholders. They should sit down with whoever heads up your marketing, people team, customer experience, and operations and create plans with each area. It may be feasible for your CIO to lead several initiatives from different functional areas of the company.

One of our biggest learning moments at MegaFood came when we decided to re-examine our flight plan and look closely at our customer; what we found was that Vibrant Vanessa had an activist side to her that we hadn't fully appreciated! She wasn't interested in her own wellness alone but in the wellness of the entire planet. When we read the new research, something seemed inescapable: our primary customer was granting us permission to not only make a better, cleaner product but also contribute our voice in making a better and cleaner world.

Sara Newmark came to MegaFood as its first vice president of social impact after leading the sustainability efforts at a major competitor. As a member of the executive leadership team, she immediately created a rationale, structure, and inspiration around our impact activities. Impact gives focus and substance to your marketing and PR, so Sara was closely involved in all these activities to look for ways to promote the company's purpose alongside its product. For example, our marketing materials shifted a bit from a focus on the quality of our supplements to the way our processes for assuring this quality supported larger aims of regenerative agriculture. From a customer point of view, choosing MegaFood was no longer simply a personal choice; it now had broader, social-impact implications.

In this regard, Sara served as an important community builder within our company and in the larger community. She also served as the focal point for our company's efforts to tap into new networks and resources that would supplement and maybe even 10x our company's best practices around impact.

Aligning Product and Purpose

Putting an impact leader on your executive team shows your team and the world you're serious about impact; it also gives your impact leader a frontline view of the company's pain points and how impact might help alleviate them. Whereas some of your operational-minded leaders might see an impact officer as a hurdle or roadblock, a good impact leader can quickly show the ways they can make life easier rather than harder.

For example, at MegaFood, those on our team in charge of turning blueberries, oranges, turmeric, and other whole foods into whole-food supplements were, to a large extent, at the mercy of the relatively few growers with whom we partnered. "From a supply chain perspective, single sourcing makes it quite difficult for a company like MegaFood," recalled Sara. "If there was a low crop in one year, it meant you either went out of stock or had to jack up the prices. And I also knew that as a company, we needed to be able to grow, and our growth was going to be limited by the carrying capacity of each farmer."

Sara helped us overcome this hurdle by creating a certification process that other growers could go through to become our partners. This increased the number of customers' lives we could impact, but it also increased the number of farmers we could support.

Externally, the 2010s were a time when the herbicide glyphosate had gained national attention after some well-publicized stories were published linking the herbicide with cancer. Given the widespread use of glyphosate in industrial farming and the close relationship between industrial-farming practices and soil degradation—a problem that certainly hit home at MegaFood as well as in the larger society—we decided to make banning the poison's use as a desiccant, or drying agent, on consumer-grade oats before harvest the issue with which we established our activist voice.

The culmination of our hard work was the successful passage by the EPA of regulations banning glyphosate as a desiccant on oats. As for the company itself, our public identification with this campaign emboldened us to begin using our external communications—our ads, website, blogs, media—to communicate our values and cause as well as promote our products.

Our larger purpose took sharper focus as a direct result of our activism. It evolved from an important but somewhat more limited goal of eliminating nutritional poverty to fixing a world that was in actual nutritional crisis. Our focus became regenerative agriculture, the practice of treating the soil with an eye toward its long-term health and biodiversity as a source of human life and all life on Earth. I bought a copy of Josh Tickell's magisterial book on regenerative agriculture called *Kiss the Ground: How the Food You Eat Can Reverse Climate Change, Heal Your Body & Ultimately Save Our World*. Everyone in the company read it, and we convened a company-wide book club to explore how we could adapt its ideas into our operations and activism. If you want to enjoy the CliffsNotes version of Tickell's book, you can watch the Netflix documentary of the same name, narrated by the inimitable Woody Harrelson.

Our company culture exploded with energy and purpose. Our creative human resources helped us transport our Zing Mojo culture outside of our four walls by recommending that we allow every employee paid time off to volunteer for an organization or cause in which they believed. Two employee-run organizations, the Culture Club and Wellness Warriors, sprang up spontaneously to feed the growing interest shown by our staff to express themselves beyond the specifications of their job descriptions.

This is an exciting time to be a part of a company—that is, when the company has taken the step to change the world in some way. You're no longer just cranking out supplements, albeit organic, non-GMO, health-supporting supplements. You're helping convince the world that regenerative agriculture offers an excellent means of pulling carbon out of the atmosphere and down into the soil where it no longer contributes to climate change but *does* contribute to healthier, more diverse soil environments. And here's the kicker: every inch deeper into the soil of activism we advanced, we also added to the stack of money we made as a business. That's right: the two went hand in hand.

And the reason wasn't hard to find: we had a deeper relationship with our customers, who had, after all, told us they wanted us to use our voice in a cause that meant something to them. Our customers, who already loved us, now had even more reason to talk about us. And those who were less passionate about our brand and might have thought *I love this multivitamin* would find themselves saying, "Oh my gosh, this company that makes my multivitamin just led a big rally in DC against glyphosate!"

Real Purpose Is Authentic to Your Brand

There is nothing phony or greenwashing about the work that you do when you scale your passion in this way. Remember, few of us who become purpose-driven leaders leap onto the stage as fully finished change-the-world actors! This role comes upon us, so to speak, in the process of wanting to make a difference, realizing that we need to be bold to do so, and then focusing like lasers on doing the right things to achieve our purpose.

Yvon Chouinard started his original climbing equipment business as a way to finance his mountaineering lifestyle and over the years recognized the interdependence he had with the natural environment that supported his passion. If you are of a certain age, you will remember the joy of receiving a Patagonia catalog because it was filled not with models showing off gear but with photos of actual users of the gear, scaling mountains, drinking coffee over an open fire with Chilean guides, and hanging off precipices in their fleeces. You wanted to be just like them! Over the years, however, Patagonia identified its mission more closely with its evolving prominence in environmental activism. No longer was it enough merely to portray its products in their proper context; instead, the company developed and published stories of Patagonia stakeholders partnering with environmentalists to preserve endangered habitats.

And you still wanted to be just like them.

Ben & Jerry's founders Ben Cohen and Jerry Greenfield began their ice cream parlor in 1978 in a run-down gas station they renovated because they couldn't afford a snazzier building. Being children of the 1960s and 1970s who grew up in Bernie Sanders's neck of the woods in Burlington, Vermont, they embraced organics, sourced locally, and gave their creative flavors names like Cherry Garcia and Chunky Monkey. But they weren't just a 1960s tribute band. And like Patagonia, as they grew and prospered, they used their resources to achieve their larger goal of linked prosperity, which has included, among other initiatives, supporting Black-owned suppliers and business partners and environmentalism.

And in an act of transparency that hits close to home to me, Patagonia has published each of its Social & Environmental Assessment Reports (SEARs) going back to 2006. I say close to home because in 2014 I launched MegaFood's Big T Transparency initiative to take leadership in establishing greater trust with retailers and consumers who felt, rightly, that supplement manufacturers weren't being honest with them about the ingredients that went into their products. The truth was that only a small percentage of brands made headlines, but they exerted an outsized negative impact on the industry.

At MegaFood, we offered live-cam open access to our New Hampshire manufacturing facilities so anyone could see what was happening at any time. We published the results of our facility audits, granting deeper access to our production processes, from ingredient sourcing to development, testing, and even auditing. In an article called "'The Big T': Major Dietary Supplement Brand Says Transparency's Time Has Come," published in *Organic Authority*, the influential Tieraona Low Dog, MD, an internationally recognized expert in the fields of dietary supplements, herbal medicine, women's health, and natural medicine, noted, "At a time of public uncertainty about the dietary supplement industry, for a company of MegaFood's stature to allow people to 'look behind the curtain' is both bold and unprecedented. This level of transparency is great for the industry and the consumer."

Dan Sullivan wrote a great book called *The 4 C's Formula* that shows how leaders can overcome fear and complacency by embracing a bolder process of goal setting exemplified by the four C's: commitment, courage, capability, and confidence. There was no question in my mind that Mega-Food experienced just such a progression. It began with our commitment to making the brand about something more than, but complementary with, profitability. Once you commit to a course of action, you build up your organization's courage to actually do something bold and impactful, which we did through our activism around glyphosate, our in-your-face (literally) advocacy of transparency, and our foray into self-managing teams using GlassFrog. And as these bold forays began to produce positive results, including steady revenue growth and the development of a top-notch leadership team, we grew more capable at scaling our purpose and profitability.

Finally, you feel confident that the decision to commit yourself to being courageous and then demonstrating you could make a difference was the right way—the only way as far you're concerned. There's a lot of positive mojo and confidence in the ability to look in the mirror and say to yourself, "This is what I want to be known for." The only thing that can match it is to look beyond the mirror to those you've had an impact on and see how they, too, are giving your purpose an entirely new set of wings. Which is the topic of our next chapter.

Lew's Tips & Resources

My dad would not be the least bit surprised that someone with fire in their belly could inspire others to take action. You may be in your business today, but I want you to take a moment right now to take a deep breath, close your eyes, and imagine what cascading impact in your company might mean.

Maxim 1: Make a Difference

- **Long-term vision:** Embrace a long-term perspective to understand the evolving needs of your customers, marketplace, and the world. This broader view enables you to identify opportunities for impactful change beyond short-term tactics.
- **Continuous learning:** Recognize the limitations of your current understanding and actively seek to expand your knowledge. As a business owner, your role is to learn how to anticipate change and innovate proactively rather than merely reacting to it.
- **Strategic partnerships:** Collaborate with industry experts and thought leaders to gain insights into emerging trends and opportunities. Leverage external expertise to drive innovation and expand your impact.

Maxim 2: Be Bold

- **Purpose-driven innovation:** Pursue bold initiatives aligned with your company's purpose, even if they involve significant risk. Embrace failure as a necessary precursor to creative breakthroughs.
- **Moonshot thinking:** Encourage bold and creative thinking within your organization by embracing the concept of "moonshots."

Pursue ambitious goals that push the boundaries of what is possible, even if they involve failure along the way.

- **Activism as a catalyst:** Harness the power of activism to amplify your company's voice and catalyze change on important issues. Use your platform to advocate for causes that align with your purpose and resonate with your customers.

Maxim 3: Do It Right

- **Impact leadership:** Establish a dedicated role within your organization focused on driving impact across all aspects of your business. Ensure that impact remains a core priority alongside other functional areas like operations, marketing, and finance.
- **Stakeholder engagement:** Engage with stakeholders across the company to develop and implement impact initiatives that align with your purpose. Foster collaboration and alignment between different functional areas to maximize the effectiveness of your impact efforts.
- **Authenticity and transparency:** Build trust with customers and stakeholders by demonstrating authenticity and transparency in your actions. Embrace initiatives like transparency reports and open access to facilities to build credibility and accountability.

Books or Articles to Consider

- *Let My People Go Surfing* by Yvon Chouinard
- *Conscious Capitalism* by John Mackey and Raj Sisodia
- *Capitalism at the Crossroads* by Stuart Hart
- *The Responsible Company* by Yvon Chouinard and Vincent Stanley
- *Firms of Endearment* by Raj Sisodia, Jagdish Sheth, and David Wolfe

- *Kiss the Ground* by Josh Tickell
- *The 4 C's Formula* by Dan Sullivan

Scale Passion Resources

- "Are You Ready to Scale?" assessment: a simple, online survey that will help you map your gaps to scaling purpose

Find a comprehensive list of resources at ScalePassion.com/Resources.

Chapter 15

Spark #4: Harness Energy

Jamie Bianchini spent years doing work that didn't have impact and feeling deeply unsatisfied. After some soul searching, a little light bulb flashed in his mind. *I know what I'll do*, Jamie thought. *I'll get a specially outfitted tandem bicycle and pedal around the world with an empty rear seat promoting peace by offering a ride to total strangers from different countries.* Thus was born Peace Pedalers.

A business major in college, Jamie set about funding his expedition. He got dozens of corporate sponsors who paid for his equipment, but he couldn't raise hard cash for simple expenses. The CEO of one technology company told him he'd love to sponsor the expedition but couldn't give him cash because Pedalers wasn't a 501c3.

"What else can you do to allow me to give you cash?" asked the CEO. "Come back to me with an idea, and I'll consider it."

So, Jamie came back to the CEO with the brilliant idea of serving as his broker with Verizon, which would pay Jamie a 10% commission every time the company paid its bill for its phone and internet services. This would help provide the cash Jamie needed and allow the technology company to make an impact by sponsoring him.

Eventually, Jamie rode with more than one thousand people all over the world and began diverting funds paid to him by Verizon to start charity projects that had an impact on thousands of people.

"To this day, kids are still graduating from the school we built in Uganda for kids with AIDS. People in Bolivia are still enjoying better health from a water project we did in Bolivia," noted Jamie with pride. "And it all came from this CEO saying yes to something he would have had to say yes to anyway, which was paying his Verizon bill."

But Jamie didn't stop there. With his wife, Christina Morales, Jamie transformed the Peace Pedaler model into a for-profit company that turns routine business expenses into transformative donations to their client's choice of nonprofit.

"We're on a mission to liberate available capital to accelerate social and environmental change," Jamie explained of the concept. "For most companies, charitable donations come out of profits after taxes, growth, and stakeholders, leaving a small amount to donate to causes that can help change the world. We realized that expenses might be a better place to look for charitable funds." They called the start-up PIE, which stands for "Purpose in Expenses."

Expenses, such as technology and utilities, comprise a huge piece of the expenses pie. Technology expenses alone add up to $4.5 trillion, say PIE's founders. Providers allow a customer to choose whether to pay them directly or through a partner. By choosing PIE as the partner, the provider pays PIE every month to maintain its account. PIE keeps half of this payment and directs the other half to its client's nonprofit of choice. This creates long-term recurring donations at no cost to the company.

PIE's pitch to clients is simple and powerful: What if every Zoom meeting or Google email you sent helped feed hungry people? You'd be okay with that, right? A company called WeHero was more than okay with it: WeHero, which connects businesses with volunteer programs, partnered with PIE to serve as its procurement partner for two of its mission-critical technology providers, Google and Zoom. With no disruption to WeHero's daily reliance on these services, PIE enabled WeHero to begin making donations to charities that have, as of this writing, paid for some three thousand meals to US families who were going hungry.

Jamie's personal purpose—if this phrase seems strange, reread chapter 2—is "to use my talents and experiences in the most beneficial way for my fellow men and women in my local and global communities by helping reduce unnecessary suffering, increase happiness, and protect the planet for future generations." He has already touched millions and now is helping other companies scale their impact.

When I look at Jamie, I see someone who has connected his personal passion to his career passion and now takes other companies that aren't seriously thinking about impact and turns them into impact companies. And that, my friends, is exponential impact.

When you feel that confidence about your purpose, you will attract others into your orbit who share a passion to make a difference. You will do this directly and indirectly. Some will share your specific passion; others will have other passions but align with your energy and focus. It's a good place to be in for a leader regardless of the kind of organization you lead.

Exponential purpose refers to the way the sparks you create by infusing your passion and purpose into your company, and which your company fans through the growth of its brand, get picked up, expanded, repurposed, and otherwise given new life by others who continue the process of expansion that transcends time and place. Exponential purpose can affect—perhaps I should say *infect*—all your stakeholders.

An example of exponential impact occurs when large strategic firms acquire small purpose-driven companies, and rather than turn them into cautious number-crunching "business units," the large firms are themselves infected by the purpose. For example, when London-based, multinational food giant Unilever acquired Ben & Jerry's in 2000, many people thought it was the end of the activist brand's social justice mission. But such was not the case. A 2016 interview between the Wharton School's Katherine Kline and Ben & Jerry's new CEO, Jostein Solheim, shared in "How Ben & Jerry's Got Bought Out Without Selling Out," in *Knowledge at Wharton*, showed how Ben & Jerry's ethos influenced Unilever even before the buyout. When Kline asked Solheim, who was an executive at Unilever prior to taking the helm at Ben & Jerry's, how the two cultures meshed, he provided an amazing insight into the fundamental way exponential purpose works. I'll reproduce the passage here:

> When companies come to the world of corporate social responsibility, they ask themselves, "What do people really care about? And how can we be a part of that?" At Ben & Jerry's, we come at it the other way. We actually ask ourselves, "What do we truly believe in—us?" And then we execute well, because we truly believe in it, and hence, convince others to join us. So that's what we mean by that: It starts with our values, and then we apply and join in movements with other partners to make change.

When Kline followed up by asking for an example, Solheim answered:

> Let's take same-sex marriage. That came on the agenda in the 1980s at Ben & Jerry's. Ben & Jerry's was one of the first companies to offer same-sex partners the same rights—health care, etc. When that started to come into the public domain and become a debate, it was very clear for the company—we couldn't just say, "You're OK if you're at Ben & Jerry's, but if you're not, you're not." So it was very natural for the employees to join in and campaign for same-sex marriage. Then, as we grew bigger, we scaled that campaign up.

And in January of 2021, Unilever announced a set of commitments to "raise the quality of life across its supply chain" through a host of measures. These included:

- Ensuring that everyone who directly provides goods and services to the company earns at least a living wage or income, by 2030.
- Spending more than $2 billion annually with suppliers owned and managed by people from underrepresented groups, by 2025.
- Pioneering new employment models for their employees, and equipping 10 million young people with essential skills to prepare them for job opportunities, by 2030.

As the company's CEO, Alan Jope, explained in a post published in 2021 on the company's website, "Without a healthy society, there cannot be a healthy business." That's language that two guys named Ben and Jerry could well appreciate.

Purpose by Any Other Name

Once you've been bitten by the purpose bug, you strive to discover new ways of cascading your purpose wherever you go. People come and go from individual organizations, but the passion for making a difference endures and makes them more likely to continue to find ways to be bold.

Sara Newmark came to MegaFood ready and willing to take the company to the next level of activism and a deeper commitment to using our voice in a great public cause. She accomplished some personal and company goals of getting MegaFood certified as a B Corp, establishing our national leadership in the effort to ban glyphosate from farming, and advancing regenerative agriculture by expanding our network of farm partners, and when she left MegaFood, she left behind a new and more purposeful culture than the one she found. And really, what more can you hope for?

"It's a great feeling to know that the programs you put in place have outlasted and are still in place," said Sara. But exponential purpose works in mysterious ways. She can look back with pride at the programs she built and the people she inspired, and when she left the company to become a partner with the founders Kristina and Brian Hall at a change-the-world business called True Grace, she was a seasoned leader who knew how to scale her purpose through her company.

That's what she's doing at True Grace, whose mission is to "provide nutrient-dense products that regenerate the health and well-being of people and planet." And if that sounds a lot like having your mission be to save the planet, so be it. But the cofounders and their small but mighty team are not contemplating their navels up there in Wisconsin. They are taking home awards like the *Nutrition Business Journal*'s Leadership and Growth Award for their dedication to regenerative agriculture.

Oh, and True Grace is also the fastest growing brand in its sector, according to the wellness-focused data company SPINS. Another line of track being laid by True Grace involves its partnership with Rodale Institute to conduct a side-by-side study of organic versus conventional farming's impact on nutrient density in crops and carbon sequestration of the soil. True Grace provides funding to Rodale's organic consulting service, which helps farmers transition to regenerative systems.

By serving on MegaFood's executive leadership team, Sara learned how the business operated from the perspectives of marketing, finance, operations, new product development, and regulatory. This not only integrated impact with the entire infrastructure of the company but also prepared Sara to become a leader of her own company where, who knows, she may one day be in a position to hire her own chief impact officer.

Ashley Larochelle came to MegaFood to be my executive assistant and left MegaFood to eventually become a vice president of people and culture at Thermacell, which manufactures area mosquito repellent devices and systems. Ashley came to MegaFood from the financial services industry looking for safe mooring in the aftermath of a rough ride through the

2008 financial crisis. "I was looking for a new kind of workplace to call home," she told me. At the time, the company was literally in a big old funky house, so she both literally and figuratively found a home.

Although the literal home-finding happened immediately, the figurative version came a bit later when, ironically, MegaFood had grown too big to be confined to a house and moved into expansive corporate headquarters with lots of manufacturing and office space. Always on the lookout for an opportunity to turn a simple event into a purpose-driven one, I wanted to invite all our stakeholders to a grand opening that would show everyone how this new facility would address our great purpose of helping cure the world's nutritional poverty.

When it came to choosing who would activate my vision for the opening, Ashley did what she always did: she raised her hand. She managed the preparation brilliantly, but on the eve of the opening, she got a call that all of us dread: her mother had been admitted to the hospital with an aneurysm that had hemorrhaged. It never occurred to me or any of the other leaders not to let Ashley drop everything at MegaFood to take care of her mother. In the end, her mother did not recover, but when Ashley returned to work, she felt a gratitude for our empathy that became the foundation for a new sense of purpose: to make the most of her time on Earth and be helpful wherever she could be.

She turned this purpose outward to her work and became my vision activation director, a position in which she participated in every important high-impact activity we did, from successfully applying for B Corp status to leading our culture club and producing the Mount Everest expedition event we used for our major company pivot. And when she left MegaFood, she did so to take on a larger impact role at Thermacell where, in memory of her mother, she helped put policies in place to extend family leave and bereavement options that, in her words, "match modern family dynamics and treat people like humans, not resources." And although still in an early stage, Thermacell is also looking at how it can help developing nations in the fight against the world's most deadly pest. That's exponential purpose in action.

Investing in Purpose

Created in 2016 by founder and CEO Hamdi Ulukaya, the Chobani Food Incubator is one of its founder's ways of sparking his exponential purpose of "transforming our food system for the betterment of our planet, our people and our communities." Through the incubator, entrepreneurs like Ethan Holmes, founder of Holmes Mouthwatering Applesauce, can vie for much-needed support, such as mentoring and funding. In fact, that's how Ethan and I originally met: I was running one of my companies, Findaway Adventures, and was looking to invest in change-the-world founders like Ethan.

As of this writing, the Chobani Food Incubator boasts a portfolio of 47 companies like Ethan's. These companies have created hundreds of jobs and hundreds of millions in growth funding that has helped boost communities in which the businesses flourish. To offer one ridiculously impressive example, in the past several years, Ethan has personally reached 50 thousand young people in communities across Ohio, Pennsylvania, and Indiana with his positive messages and practical curriculum aimed at helping more young people living in underserved communities explore entrepreneurism.

Second Time Founders (2TF) is an exemplary business that focuses on exponential impact work within a different industry—technology. Founded by Kwiri Yang, a serial entrepreneur experienced in the pressure, stress, and isolation often faced by Silicon Valley founders, 2TF provides a range of personal and leadership development programs that utilize conscious leadership and other practices to support founders.

2TF also offers a network of founders who provide mutual support and share their experiences to learn from one another. The demand for

2TF's services has risen dramatically as investors and tech founders alike recognize the need to develop leadership and interpersonal and soft skills alongside technical innovation.

Kwiri notes that investors want assurance that the leaders receiving their substantial investments possess both leadership and innovation capabilities. "Silicon Valley has many brilliant individuals who understand quantum physics and artificial intelligence but struggle to communicate their intentions and values effectively," Kwiri observes. "They are highly intellectual individuals who, when threatened, resort to stonewalling. The recent AI controversy and blowout at the prominent AI start-up are predictable consequences of these types of issues."

More than 350 leaders have enrolled in programs like those offered by 2TF, demonstrating their commitment to addressing these concerns. One such founder, Diego Saez Gil, joined the 2TF community after exiting two companies and engaging in deep introspection with other founders to share his realizations and reflections of his identity beyond entrepreneurship. His journey led him to discover the interconnectedness of life and the importance of vulnerability and truth in leadership.

"There are countless networking spaces where everyone discusses their Silicon Valley success stories," Diego said. "While it's great to celebrate accomplishments, we also need spaces to share our failures, doubts, and inner journeys. As founders, we can benefit from speaking a different language with one another, focusing on the heart rather than solely on success and wealth."

Diego shifted his focus to creating work environments where people could thrive and supporting flourishing communities. He shared, "I learned to align myself with a larger purpose, resulting in greater happiness and sustainable motivation. When you work for something bigger than yourself, things flow more easily." Diego's current venture, Pachama, is a company dedicated to restoring nature through the creation of a market for forest carbon offsets.

To Andrew Chomer, managing partner at Integrated, which is a venture capital firm that invests in the emerging mental health and health care technology sectors, the future is all about the lens we choose to put on what matters most. Andrew says that while return on capital is a good measure of external success, his firm looks at a broader set of criteria to determine which companies to invest in. Integrated creates a balance of founder/leadership criteria, product-to-market fit, and key performance metrics while it incorporates a wider range of softer factors to determine whether a company is both a viable investment and has the opportunity to create a positive, lasting impact on the world—beginning with the world inside its four walls.

In these companies, a certification as a B Corp and its ESG policies creates value for multiple stakeholders and serves as signs that a company might very well have its head and heart in the right places, but Integrated is doctrinaire about variables such as these. More important, Andrew says, is that the company is striving to improve lives both internally and externally. Andrew explains,

> Capital has energy. When money comes into the picture, it's too easy to forget what you stood for once upon a time and focus exclusively on profits. But profits and purpose are not mutually exclusive lenses through which to see a business. When Facebook began, its primary purpose of sharing and connecting people around the world was at the core of its mission. Then, as more capital gets infused into the business, it shifts to monetizing eyeballs and it starts to lose sight of its core mission. There's always that tension between what's best for the company profits and what's best for the people who work at the company and use its services.

Andrew is one of a growing number of investors who are asking business owners to think about their responsibilities in a broader way that asks questions like the following: How do you treat the people the right way? How do you build good leadership teams? How do you build in allowances for difficult times or moments that happen in people's lives, helping them grow as individuals while building a company that continues to thrive and impact others outside the company?

We might call it Capitalism 3.0, or *new capitalism*, an approach to running a profitable company that places mindfulness high on the list of desirable leadership traits. There are many ways of developing greater mindfulness as a leader, and many tools and techniques to draw from. In addition to conscious leadership, there are Enneagram and other personality assessment tools you can adapt to your own organization to better understand your and your teammates' triggers and fuels. You can participate in a program at the Hendricks Institute, founded by the psychologist and teacher Gay Hendricks, who also wrote *The Big Leap*, an essential book for mindful leaders. Or you can read books such as those mentioned in Lew's Tips and at scalepassion.com/resources.

One of the things Andrew looks at when evaluating a company is "the amount of fear or love within an organization." He looks at how a firm communicates, where employees' energy comes from, and how much real agency employees feel in their work. "We look deeper than simply whether a company is carbon neutral or has the right employee benefits," he said. "We value whether leaders and their teams are leading from a place of love or showing up with a deep sense of fear or insecurity within the culture. And we believe that the former is much more consistent with building a thriving environment."

Impact Is Agnostic

Capitalism 3.0 or change-the-world business isn't left wing or right wing, Democrat or Republican, or any other kind of polarizing doctrine. There is no dotted line you have to sign on pledging your allegiance to any single great cause—other than the one you care about—to begin the process of unleashing your purpose, building it into the fabric of your business, and radiating it out into the world.

I love a company called Black Rifle Coffee, whose mission is "to serve coffee and culture to people who love America." Founded in 2014 by US Army Green Beret Evan Hafer, the company describes itself as "a Veteran-founded business operated by principled men and women who honor those who protect, defend and support our country." Black Rifle hires veterans, trains them to become entrepreneurs in their own right, and produces content about hunting, fishing, and outdoor adventure through its Free Range American platform. Its philanthropic arm, the nonprofit Black Rifle Coffee Company Fund, engages with local communities and partners with organizations to support veterans, first responders, and their families by giving them the care and resources they need to thrive in their communities.

The point is one person with a burning passion and purpose can set off ripples of impact that radiate far and wide! Whether it's about impacting climate change, supporting farmers or veterans, or simply supporting your community, you can build a company that is likely to do even more good than you can dream of.

Lew's Tips & Resources

Listen, deep down there is a kernel in everyone who wants to do something in this world, small or big, to make some sort of difference. These actions, no matter how small, make a ripple. My dad's pouring his knowledge and experience into me so many years ago had an impact on me. What impact might you have?

Maxim 1: Make a Difference

- **Purpose as a magnet:** Confidence in purpose attracts like-minded individuals, fostering a community dedicated to making a difference.
- **Exponential impact:** Purpose-driven actions have a multiplier effect, influencing stakeholders beyond immediate circles and creating broader societal change.
- **Investing in purpose:** Initiatives like the Chobani Food Incubator empower purpose-driven entrepreneurs to effect meaningful change and positively impact communities.

Maxim 2: Be Bold

- **Direct and indirect influence:** Purpose-driven business owners attract others who align with their energy and focus, creating a powerful force for change.
- **Exponential impact:** Purpose-driven companies influence larger organizations and shape corporate culture, leading to significant societal impact.
- **Mindful leadership:** Mindful leadership is so important in Capitalism 3.0, where leaders prioritize values like empathy, authenticity,

and love over mere profit, fostering a healthier work environment and aligning with broader societal goals.

Maxim 3: Do It Right

- **Personal transformation:** Personal growth driven by purpose, showcased by individuals like Sara Newmark and Ashley Larochelle, leave lasting legacies beyond their tenure in any one organization.
- **Impact is agnostic:** Purpose-driven businesses transcend political divides and ideological differences, focusing on shared goals of making a positive impact on the world.

Other Resources and Inspiration to Consider

- Chobani Food Incubator (chobani.com/impact/incubator)
- True Grace (truegracehealth.com)
- Thermacell (thermacell.com)
- Second Time Founders (secondtimefounders.com)
- Cloverleaf personality testing (cloverleaf.me)
- Enneagram Institute (enneagraminstitute.com)
- Hendricks Institute (hendricks.com)

Scale Passion Resources

- "Are You Ready to Scale?": a simple, online survey that will help you map your gaps to scaling purpose

Find a comprehensive list of resources at ScalePassion.com/Resources.

Epilogue

Closing this book is bittersweet for me. As I reflect on the journey we've taken together, my mind naturally drifts back to my dad, Lew Craven. His story is one of resilience, purpose, and unwavering passion—a story that deserves to be shared.

When I was just a child, Dad faced a daunting battle with Hodgkin's disease. But he refused to let it define him. With courage and determination, he conquered his illness and emerged stronger than ever. Instead of letting adversity defeat him, he channeled his experience into a mission to support others through their struggles with grief.

With a master's in grief counseling, he dedicated himself to serving those in need, volunteering, and ultimately working directly with Life-Path Hospice in Tampa, Florida, and cofounding Camp Circle of Love—a sanctuary for children who have lost a parent. He later went on to become a professor, teaching a new generation of counselors. His impact was profound, touching the lives of countless individuals and families.

Throughout my life, Dad was my steadfast support. From cheering me on at sports events to guiding me through life's milestones—new jobs, terminations, my marriage to my wonderful wife, two amazing daughters—he was always there, leading by example and instilling in me the values of purpose and passion.

Together with my mom, my dad built a life filled with love, purpose, and meaning. Their marriage of more than 50 years is a testament to the power of commitment and partnership. And even in his final days, he continued to inspire, leaving behind a legacy of compassion and service that will endure for generations to come. My mom and I recently presented the Lew Craven Volunteer of the Year Award at the same camp he helped found.

My dad may not have been a CEO or a founder of a large company, but his impact was immeasurable. He taught me that purpose knows no bounds and that each of us has the power to make a difference in the lives of others.

So, as we part ways, I carry with me the lessons learned from Lew's life—a legacy of purpose, passion, and unwavering commitment. And I hope that his spirit continues to inspire us all to do it right, be bold, and to make a difference in the world around us.

Thank you for joining me on this journey. May we all strive to honor Lew's memory by living our lives with purpose and passion, just as he did.

Acknowledgments

A s I reflect on the journey of writing this book, I am filled with gratitude for the many individuals who have supported, inspired, and guided me along the way. This book would not have been possible without the contributions of so many exceptional people.

First and foremost, I owe a debt of gratitude to Dave Moore—without him, there would be no book. His ability to capture my voice, thoughts, inspirations, and approaches on the page is nothing short of a superpower. His probing questions and deep understanding allowed this book to come to life and deliver its full potential. Thank you, Dave, for your partnership on this adventure. A huge thank-you also to Katie Dickman, our editor, and Matt Holt, our editor-in-chief, as well as the entire team at Matt Holt Books and BenBella. Your wisdom and approach were instrumental in making this process seamless.

To my family, the foundation of everything I do: My father, whose passing I have written about extensively, was and remains the major influence for this book. His example of service and passion is an everlasting beacon in my own journey. My mother, Patsy, whose unconditional love and resilience continue to inspire me, and my wife, Dianna, who is not only my best friend but also the person who continually teaches me about integrity and helps me grow each day. To my two daughters, Emily and

Paige, whose choices in life continually teach me the power of individuality and the importance of following one's dreams.

Professionally, I must express my deepest thanks to Cody Thompson of The Table Group for his introductions and invaluable guidance. I am also eternally grateful to Jim Dethmer, Diana Chapman, and Erica Schreiber of The Conscious Leadership Group for their 15 Commitments Coach Certification program and training. Your teachings have radically changed my life and propelled me to pursue integrity and purpose with everything I have. A special shout-out to the remarkable individuals who walked this conscious leadership path with me: Andrew, Jason, Dolores, Sierra, Schlaf, Jim F, Anjani, Ashwini, Nanci, Stephanie, Beerit, Michael, Nichol, Samantha, Matt, Silvana, Susie, and countless others.

My path has been shaped by the incredible people I've worked with over the years. I want to thank my team at ScalePassion—Nick, Steve, Lainy, Rhonda, and Bethany—for helping simplify and dial in the concepts and approaches in this book. To the inspirational entrepreneurs I had the privilege of working alongside—Jordan Rubin of Garden of Life, Carl Jackson of MegaFood, and Jethren Phillips of New Organic Ventures—you were the models and valued companions as we navigated the landscape of growth and impact. I feel deep gratitude for the inspiring companies that trusted my small company, ScalePassion, to work out our approaches with them—Momentous, Joyride, Total Fire Protection, Infinity Drain, Carbe Diem, CellX, Oxford Healthspan, Thermacell, and Timberlane—without your partnership this book would not be what it is. A special mention to Dave Tiley, the first Chairman of the Board and Operating Partner I ever worked with, for your wisdom, insights, and growth mindset. To the many vice presidents who supported me during my tenure as CEO, including Jean, Dan, Steve, Elsa, Sara, Ed, Mark, Jim, Ed, Jason, Rob, James, Stephanie, Roger, David, Traci, Craig, Richard, Gary, Dana, and Richard—you made the impact and success possible. And a special, heartfelt thanks to Ashley Larochelle, my Vision Activation Director at MegaFood, without whom few of our innovative approaches would have succeeded.

A special thank-you to the thought leaders and authors who influenced my approach. Patrick Lencioni, your simplicity, creativity, and practical insights were paramount. Thanks also to Jim Collins, James Clear, Tim Ferriss, Anthony Bourdain, John Doerr, Dan Sullivan, Steven Pressfield, Ryan Holiday, Gay and Kathlyn Hendricks, Stephen Covey, Mark Manson, Seth Godin, Clayton M. Christensen, John Kotter, Malcolm Gladwell, and so many others. A special appreciation for Michael Porter for the amazing live seminar on Creating Shared Value at Harvard Business School, which was so influential and pivotal.

I also want to acknowledge Doug Abrams for his mentorship and encouragement, and Aaron Bartz for his decades of friendship, inspiration, and wisdom. Your support for this book and ScalePassion has been immeasurable.

My spiritual journey has been a guiding light in my quest to scale impact. From Rick Warren's *The Purpose Driven Life* to Jim Dethmer, Diana Chapman and Kaley Warner Klemps's *The 15 Commitments of Conscious Leadership*, these works have reinforced my search, exploration, and expression of purpose. I want to extend my gratitude to the spiritual thinkers who have influenced my path, including Sam Harris, Michael Singer, Richard Rohr, C. S. Lewis, Stephen Cope, and Jed McKenna.

To the reader, thank you for being on this odyssey of exploration toward living a life of fulfillment and impact. I encourage you to stay on track and continue pulling on that string toward identifying, exploring, and living your purpose—no matter how big or small the impact may seem.

Finally, writing this book has been a beautiful exploration of my life, my quest toward purpose, and an inventory of impact and vision. It has solidified my commitment to scaling impact, both personally and for the leaders and businesses I have the privilege to work with.

To everyone mentioned here and the countless others who have touched my life in ways big and small—thank you. This book is a testament to the collective effort of many, and I am deeply grateful for your contributions.

About the Authors

Rob Craven is a purpose-driven CEO, founder, and author dedicated to radically evolving capitalism by connecting personal purpose to business success. As the former CEO of MegaFood and Garden of Life, Rob led both companies to achieve rapid, profitable growth, B-Corporation status, and successful financial exits. Under his leadership, Garden of Life was ranked #14 on the Inc. 500 List of Fastest-Growing Companies, and MegaFood earned spots on multiple "Best Place to Work" lists.

Recognized as one of the Top Conscious Business Leaders of 2018 by Conscious Company Media, Rob's leadership has been celebrated for its focus on transparency, innovation, and building award-winning cultures.

With over two decades of experience working with entrepreneurs, private equity, and large multinational companies, Rob has become a trusted advisor to high-growth, impact-driven businesses. As the founder of ScalePassion, he now helps business leaders harness purpose to scale their companies and create meaningful, sustainable change in the world.

Rob's personal mission is to empower leaders to connect their personal purpose with their business purpose, enabling them to radiate impact across their organizations and beyond. His passion for transformative leadership has made him a sought-after speaker, coach, and thought leader in the realm of social impact and conscious business.

Rob lives with his family in Florida and continues to inspire and instruct leaders around the world through his writing, speaking, and hands-on consulting.

Dave Moore is a writer and editor who has written extensively on business and culture. He has ghostwritten and edited dozens of articles for *Forbes*, *CEO*, and other publications, as well as four books including one *Wall Street Journal* bestseller. After earning a bachelor's degree in English from the University of Rochester and a doctorate in American Civilization from Brown University, he began writing on a wide range of topics including contemporary American culture, leadership, biography, and the nexus of sports and leadership.

HELP
US
CHANGE
THE
WORLD

Join the ScalePassion community and help us make this world a better place.

Follow this link for book resources, newsletter sign-up, coaching, and more.

scalepassion.com/resources